G000129077

INTRODUCTION

I wrote my first travel report on the *Trans-Siberian* railway line at the beginning of September 2014. I had left the city of Irkutsk in Siberia twenty-four hours earlier, commencing my sixty-nine-hour journey to Vladivostok, the most Eastern city of Russia. I was getting bored sitting on the train and so, after a few glasses of vodka with Sasha, the old man who was sleeping in the bunk under mine, I began to write in my notebook. What followed was a summary of observations, extrapolated from my diary, about the first month of travel, focusing on the most amusing anecdotes and reflections on the most striking cultural and environmental differences I discovered traveling overland, at that time from Italy to the Sea of Japan.

I had a Russian sim in my phone at that moment, given to me a few days before by a Siberian girl who, "fallen in love" with me, was more than determined not to lose my track. Thanks to that sim card and the consequent internet connection, I had been able to post the report I had just written on *Facebook*, eager for friends and relatives to read the weird situations I had experienced in my first month of travel.

The outcome turned out to be dramatically different from what I had expected. Not only did many of my acquaintances write to me in response, but also dozens of people encouraged me to continue writing. Friends who I had not seen for years began to contact me - primary school companions reappeared from the intricacies of the web adding me on *Facebook*. It was when several girls who, until recently, did not even care of me, began to ask me how I was, I realized the significance of my post and that I had to keep writing, even though during high school my best Italian classwork was worth only a miserable score.

At the time, September 2014, I had been traveling for a month with the purpose to reach Australia by land using only public transport. I wanted to get there by (for) Christmas, so I expected to write another four or five reports, about one a month.

At the time I did not yet know that once I reached Australia, I would stop there to work for a year.

At the time I did not yet know that after a year of working in the land of kangaroos, I would return to Italy by hitchhiking, starting from Singapore.

At the time I did not yet know that back in Italy after more than two years travelling, in December 2016 I would decide to move to China to work as a teacher in a public primary school.

At the time I did not yet know that once my work contract in China was complete, I would return to Italy by bicycle, starting from Tibet.

At the time, after writing the first report, I didn't conceive that I would come to write twenty more in the next four years. I was crossing Asia by land and it already seemed like a colossal adventure to me. I couldn't have known that I would do it twice more!

FROM ITALY TO INDONESIA USING PUBLIC TRANSPORT

The first trip started from Italy in the summer of 2014. Life in Milano, working as basketball coach, was pleasant, stable and full of satisfaction but it began to feel monotonous and with fewer fresh emotions. At twenty-six I began to struggle seeing myself stuck in that context for the rest of my life. So, without giving it much thought, I decided to quit my job and take a "sabbatical year" to follow my biggest passion - traveling. I did not want to be a tourist; I wanted to take a long trip, building contacts with local people, and I wanted to visit places as most preserved as possible. I was not running away from home and I did not even care about getting out of my "comfort zone". I was just looking for adventures and strong emotions. I was being led by the irresistible desire to travel. Just it!

I left home in Milan on the 6th of August 2014 with the intention of reaching Indonesia by land with public transport. From there I planned to fly to Australia to earn back the money I had spent during the trip. I would then return to Italy to continue the life I had temporarily interrupted.

At least that was what I believed.

Prior to this trip I had already experienced some adventurous travelling, but this time I had no plans and I was about to embark on a trip that would take me to Asia for the first time in my life... I left with a small backpack and a small budget but with an incredible desire of freedom.

Route Map: Italy, Austria, Czech Republic, Poland, Belarus, Russia, Mongolia, Russia, China, Hong Kong, Macau, China, Vietnam, Laos, Cambodia, Thailand, Malaysia, Singapore, Indonesia.

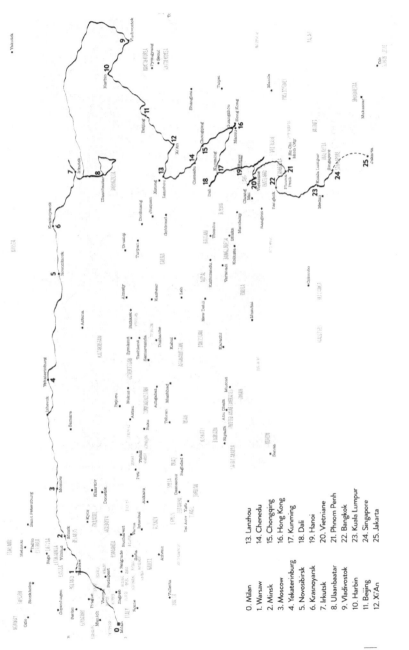

0. Milan
1. Warsaw
2. Minsk
3. Moscow
4. Yekaterinburg
5. Novosibirsk
6. Krasnoyarsk
7. Irkutsk
8. Ulaanbaatar
9. Vladivostok
10. Harbin
11. Beijing
12. Xi'An

13. Lanzhou
14. Chenedu
15. Chongqing
16. Hong Kong
17. Kunming
18. Dali
19. Hanoi
20. Vietniane
21. Phnom Penh
22. Bangkok
23. Kuala Lumpur
24. Singapore
25. Jakarta

11

FIRST TRAVEL REPORT
AUGUST - SEPTEMBER 2014

Nations crossed: Belarus, Russia, Mongolia

9 nights spent on the train

12 people who hosted me in their homes

21 nights in which I stayed in the homes of my hosts

30+ people who offered me a meal, a ride, a cigarette or some other gift of kindness

65 hours, the longest route by train

150+ hours, the total amount of time spent on the Trans-Siberian trains

Some considerations on the places seen:

- A girl in Siberia asked me if sea water is truly salty.

- In Mongolia, the cure for high blood pressure involves putting flower petals into their shoes.

- Crossing the road in Ulan Bator, the capital of Mongolia, has been one of the most dangerous experiences of my life.

- In Russia it is forbidden to smoke on the train unless you buy a lottery ticket, at which point you can smoke as much as you want. Obviously, everybody buys the ticket so they can smoke, without ever checking if they have won.

- In Buryat villages, home of the indigenous Siberian population, there is no asphalt and no pottery - so no roads and no bathrooms.

- The girls in Mongolia are very pretty but they don't like hairy men; while the girls in Siberia are even more beautiful and they love hairy men. I have been pretty lucky this time!

- The most famous Italian in Russia, after the singer Toto Cotugno, is the football player Gigi Buffon. Some nostalgic people have also mentioned to me: Cabrini, Zoff and Rossi, former Italian footballers from the eighties.

- 50% of Russians are nostalgic for communism and hate the former president Gorbachev and Perestroika. The other 50% thanks Gorbachev and love Perestroika.

- Lake Baikal in Siberia is as long as the distance between Milan to Naples (636km), as wide as Milan to Bergamo(40km) and as deep as seventeen football fields.

- In Mongolia it is believed that if a bee makes a nest in your house you will become rich... so I had to spend two nights with a bee flying in my tent, with the fear of being stung.

- Lukashenko's dictatorship makes Minsk the cleanest, the most organized and the safest capital city I have ever visited. However, some Belarusian journalists and political opposition activists have ended up on the "missing persons list" in the last two decades.

- In Minsk, if you ride a motorcycle you cannot exceed the speed limits during the day but at night you can do whatever you want. The law says it: after 24.00 I have only seen people boosting.

- In Russia, if you are Russian, museums are cheaper. In Mongolia, if you're not Mongolian, everything is more expensive.

- The *"Lonely Planet Siberia"* defined the city of Krasnoyarsk as "the Paris of Siberia" ... Well! They have been much too generous!

- For the first time in my life I met a true Buddhist and for the first time in my life I have been stopped by killing a mosquito that had its eye on my calf!

- After a month in Siberia I know 5-6 words in Russian but anyone who has hosted me can say "Minchia" (a pretty elegant way to say *WTF* in Italian).

- The Novosibirsk Province is as big as France. The municipality of Novosibirsk is as large as 20 Italian cities.

- Seeing someone of African background in Siberia is almost impossible. The only one I saw was dressed like 50 Cent and photographed by passers-by.

- In Mongolia basketball is very popular. You can see a lot of kids playing basketball, but you can see many more kids playing archery.

- In Mongolia I was lucky enough to work with a nomad family. My job? Collecting their yak's excrement to be used during the winter to set the fire for cooking and warming the tent.

- A month spent in Russia and I've not spent a single euro for accommodation - I have been hosted by someone every single night! Sometimes I have been hosted by people from *Couchsurfing*, sometimes by people randomly met in the street or on the train. I have been amused by Russian hospitality.

- The nomad family I lived with in Mongolia had 43 yaks... 42 female yaks and 1 male yak. I have never envied anybody so much as I envied that male yak!

- On the *Trans-Siberian* train, your seat neighbor may vary between the most beautiful girl you've ever seen and a fat, alcoholic Russian who farts continuously. The advantage (or rather, disadvantage in the latter case) is that on the Trans-Siberian you have to spend at least 50 hours stuck next to them... You start believing in fate!!!

To watch the video *"Crossing Asia by land – Chapter one – Belarus, Mongolia, Russia"* about this report, search the link or scan the QR code with your device.

www.youtube.com/watch?v=H-sK7bvd2i4

SECOND TRAVEL REPORT
SEPTEMBER - OCTOBER 2014

Nations crossed: Russia, China, Hong Kong

1 the number of insects that I have been made to eat

4 people have hosted me

7 nights I have been hosted in total

7 nights spent on a train

17 nights spent in 9 different hostels

1 person who has cheated me

15+ people who tried to cheat me in vain (being silly once was more than enough)

34 years of life lost when, in Beijing, the ATM did not return my credit card, my train was leaving in twenty minutes and no one spoke my language within fifty kilometers

100+ people who asked me for a picture

Some considerations on China:

- Chinese communist politics makes Chinese people the most serene and happy nation that I have ever met, but also certainly the least creative and imaginative.

- Many Chinese are not aware of the fact that Chinese people live in countries across the world.

- Beijing is so polluted that I have not seen the sun for eight days.

- The most famous Italian in China is... none! So, for many Chinese, I have become the most famous Italian person. I fear that my wild beard, my travel-stained T-shirts and solo-traveler condition must not be giving a good impression of Italian people!

- My Chinese name is Lou Lou. It sounds very effeminate, but in China "piano" (floor) is "lou", consequently "Piani" (my surname, plural of floor) becomes "Lou Lou".

- When informing a Tibetan monk "I am Italian" and he replied: "ah Italy... Balotelli (an Italian silly footballer)!" for a moment I missed the "old time" when Italy was associated with *Mafia*.

- In China people do not vote... there is only one party. But, even if it looks like an impossible concept for Western countries, in China it seems to work pretty well. Economically, the country is growing fast and citizens appear to be happy and satisfied.

- In Chinese vocabulary there is no word to say "comfortable" and I have seen this when travelling by train or bus!

- In China, spitting everywhere is normal. The main problem is that the loading phase is emphasized with sounds that I had never heard before!

- In China, burping everywhere is normal and they are very talented in doing so.

- The Great Wall of China is by far the most incredible construction I've ever seen.

- In China the numbers shown with the fingers are different from ours, like 10 for example is done by crossing the indices. During the first few weeks it was really hard to understand the cost of food.

- It's very uncommon for a Chinese person to ask "why," especially when talking to parents and teachers. They believe everything that is taught them without questioning the reason.

- Chinese population is certainly more than the one billion seven hundred million that they want us to believe.

- The concept of personal space when you are in line or on buses does not exist there.

- Basketball is very popular in China but the technical, tactical and even athletic level is quite poor.

- When two individuals are in a relationship, it's pretty common for the boy to hold his girlfriend's purse.

- I've spent my first night in China at Harbin University - it houses 30,000 students in the dormitories (8 people in each room). In the evening I expected there to be parties... Instead, at 10 pm all the students were already in bed! Someone even told me it's very bad for a male student to be found with a girl on the university campus

- In China when a boy dates a girl, he will probably marry her.

- The need for work is so urgent that people seem to be encouraged to throw rubbish on the ground so that individuals can be hired to pick it up.

- After a dinner at any Chinese restaurant in Milan I have experienced a stomach ache for a week. Here in China I've eaten all kinds of poultry, pork noses and other crazy stuff and I never had a problem.

- On "third class" trains in Russia on the cheapest night wagon there are 60 beds and 2 toilets for 60 people. In China on third class trains there are 118 seats (you sleep sitting) and 2 bathrooms for about 130 people. Whoever does not have a seat camps somewhere on the floor. Of course, everyone is smoking and, in some provinces, even spitting is kind of common.

- At the food market in Chengdu, along with tomatoes and apples you can also find turtles, snakes, frogs... all alive.

- Chinese children run around without a nappy, they all have a hole in their trousers from which they can poo at any time and in any place.

- In China, many pedestrian crossings are without traffic lights, so it is your self-preservation instinct alone that tells you when to cross.

- The width of China occupies a space that should have at least four time zones. Instead, they have one. At the beginning of September at 6.30 pm it's dark.

- It seems that bus drivers in China are not paid for how many hours their shift lasts but for how many cars they can overtake.

- On Chinese maps a city depicted as big as we show a little city on Italian maps has at least ten million inhabitants.

- Communist politics is probably the only way to manage such a large nation.

- Many Tibetans have so little beard that instead of using a razor they use tweezers.

- China is a magical country and the Chinese people are incredibly cheerful, friendly and respectful.

To watch the video *"Crossing Asia by land – Chapter two – China, Hong Kong"* about this report, search the link or scan the QR code with your device.

www.youtube.com/watch?v=3S-W0V2puso

THIRD TRAVEL REPORT
OCTOBER - NOVEMBER 2014

Nations crossed: China, Hong Kong, Macao, Vietnam, Laos

1 night slept at the beach

1 night began by sleeping on a bench in a public garden in China and ended up in a luxury downtown apartment

1 night spent in a boat

1 night spent in a tent in Laos

1 night on a stilt house (also in Laos)

4 nights spent on trains

4 nights spent on coaches

18 nights spent in 12 different hostels

10 vehicles used to travel- train, bus, night bus (with beds), tuk tuk, motorcycle, scooter, raft, kayak, ship, car

Some gems from China and South East Asia:

- In the Chinese countryside 99% of the clothing is fake. It is common to see young Chinese teenagers with tremendous shirts branded with fake names as ArNaMi or Adidos.

- Hong Kong is a spectacular city but if you are travelling cheap with a €15 daily budget, it's definitely not for you.

- Macau is nothing special... it's like China but with lots of Casinos and even a fake Venetian San Marco square, which I refused to visit.

- During the Chinese National Holiday at the beginning of October, the greatest migration of human history takes place every year. One billion people travel to the most famous places in China.

- If I have understood correctly, Laotian language is very easy because it has very limited vocabulary. For example, "ice" is called hard water, "bathroom" is home water, while "eclipse" is frog eats moon.

- The lianas in the forest of Southeast Asia can hold up to four people (even 6/7 if they are locals).

- The flexibility of the Chinese is just incredible, if they do not have a seat they can stay in a full squat position for hours.

- In Kunming, China, I met a Buddhist who spoke English for the first time. In just four hours this man both slaughtered me at ping pong and overturned all my most important concepts and beliefs about life.

- The streets of Hanoi, the capital of Vietnam, are so messed up that me and a Canadian guy got lost despite possessing a map and his GPS.

- I arrived in Vietnam and changed one hundred euros. The guy at the exchange gave me two-million-five hundred thousand Vietnamese dollars.

- The border between Laos and Vietnam is the most bombed area in history. This was kindly pointed out to me by the bus driver while I was entering the vegetation looking for a hidden bush to poop... I immediately turned around!

- In Laos, in every hostel and in many clubs, it is compulsory to take off shoes to enter.

- At the Hue market in Vietnam I had lunch at a table with two Americans in their sixties. During the meal I discovered that it was their second visit to Vietnam. On their first trip, forty years ago, they were not there on vacation.

- The most famous Italian in Vietnam is clearly Roberto Baggio (a famous footballer who follows Buddhism).

- In the forest in Vietnam more than once I confused a butterfly with a bird.

- In Laos it is considered serious if a man and a woman kiss or shake hands in public places. Even in the rooms of some hostels I found signs explicitly noting that it was "forbidden to have sex".

- The jungle in Vietnam is so dense that you understand easily why the Americans lost the war.

- In Laos they use the banana leaf as a smoking paper for rolling tobacco.

- In Vietnam when it starts raining if you do not find a shelter within fifteen seconds you find yourself more wet than if you had a bucket of water tipped over your head.

- In sixty days between China, Vietnam and Laos, I have never seen a person pissed off or fighting with someone else. Indeed, especially in Laos, everyone is always smiling!

- Pubs and bars in Laos all close at 11.30pm, while the restaurants generally shut down at 8.30pm/9.00pm. The hairdressers, however, are open until 10 pm and there is always at least one customer.

- In Laos no one owns a watch, and, in their vocabulary, there is no word to express "stress".

- Bananas are eight to ten centimeters long... and they suck.

- In Laos the most popular sport among the village kids is football-tennis played with a strange ball made of strands of bamboo reeds.

- In villages in Laos you can find families of 50 people - generally 40 of them are children.

- Life expectancy in Laos is fifty-six years, in fact it is impossible to see an elderly person.

- In Laos and Vietnam there is no McDonald's, Burger King or KFC.

- In Laos the official religion is Buddhism but in small villages they believe more in ghosts and witches.

- The propaganda of the Communist Popular Party in Vietnam and Laos is similar to the Soviet propaganda of the 1950s and 1960s.

- In a village in the forest in Laos, at my request for food (mimicking the gesture of eating) I got, instead of food, a giant joint (always rolled in the banana leaf).

To watch the video *"Crossing Asia by land – Chapter three – Southeast Asia"* about this report, search the link or scan the QR code with your device.

www.youtube.com/watch?v=Gyp8RJwQJkl

FOURTH TRAVEL REPORT
NOVEMBER - DECEMBER 2014

Nations crossed: Laos (last two days), Cambodia, Thailand, Malaysia (arrived the day before yesterday)

2 nights spent on buses

5 different islands I camped on, four in Thailand and one in Laos (on Mekong river)

10 nights spent in bungalows by the sea

12 kg lost since I left Italy

13 different bungalows or hostels where I have slept

18 nights spent in hostels

20+ species of animals seen in the wild, including a shark, sea turtle, giant lizard, freshwater dolphins and different types of monkeys

40+ kg of rice eaten in the last month... I cannot eat it anymore!

50+ liters of beer consumed in a month between Laos, Cambodia and Thailand (at least 30 only in Thailand)

Some considerations on the countries just visited:

- In Cambodia on a 12-seater minivan I found myself amongst 19 people... One girl even sat on the driver's seat between him and the door.

- In Cambodia almost all the kids wear football shirts - Chelsea, Liverpool and Barcelona. The worst I saw was a boy with the Inter Milano shirt of... Giorgio Chiellini (Italian player, who has never played for Inter Milano).

- The law in Cambodia for motorcycles and scooters requires the driver to wear a helmet while the second and third passengers can ride without it. Having a fourth passenger is discouraged but not prohibited.

- Basketball in Cambodia is very poor. Martial arts and cockfights are much more popular.

- In Thailand Muay Thai is very popular, but very often in the villages you can see children playing bowls using slippers instead of bowls.

- Cambodians are spectacular. They always smile and they are very kind. As soon as I arrived in the city of Kratie, a guy in a bar lent me his bike to go and get some cash at the ATM. Because the ATM was not working the waitress gave me money for dinner and for the hostel.

- In Thailand it is very cheap... But I do not know how I spent more money in fifteen days in Thailand than in thirty-five days in China... I guess I had too many beers!

- When you rent a bungalow or a single tent in areas near the jungle, you know that you will have to share your room. Generally, you will share it with a dozen mosquitoes, a couple of cockroaches and at least one spider... If you are unlucky you also get a gecko, which, although it is the nicest of all, when it begins to croak at night, the sound is very annoying.

- If someone tells you to pay attention to transsexuals in Bangkok, listen to him ...

- In Thailand, on the boat between the mainland and the island of Ko Tao, the sea was quite rough... After a while many tourists began to vomit around me. I was very calm, thinking "it must be nothing extraordinary". When the Thai woman sitting next to me put on her life jacket and started to cry, I started to worry too.

- In the seventies Cambodians suffered a genocide very similar to the Jewish one. The only difference is that it was perpetrated by a Cambodian himself. Pol Pot, a member of the Communist party, killed all the people who were educated - all the teachers, journalists, doctors, and so forth, condemning Cambodia to a level of poverty and illiteracy that is still evident today.

- There is no railway line in Laos.

- The most expensive "restaurant" I've eaten in Thailand is McDonald's.

- In Phnom Penh, every ten meters you are stopped by a taxi driver (who drives a tuk tuk, a particular three-wheeled form of transport). The conversation typically goes like this:

Taxi driver: tuk tuk?

Me: no thanks

Taxi driver: marijuana?

Me: no thanks

Taxi driver: cocaine?

Me: no thanks

Taxi driver: bum bum?

Me: hahahahha

- In villages in Thailand they have no landfill. At dusk each family piles all their waste in front of the house and sets fire to it.

- In Laos and Cambodia there are no coins, only banknotes.

- In Malaysia, Muslims live according to the Islamic religion with enviable rigor, consistency and dedication, and I could feel the interior peace they receive from prayers. These people really get up at five to pray every morning.

- Seeing Christmas trees and hearing in the streets "We wish you a Merry Christmas" while you're walking in a tank top, and flip-flops is a weird experience.

- From the banks of the Mekong River, especially in Southern Laos and Cambodia, I have seen flocks of dolphins (in a river!).

- The capital of Cambodia is a beautiful city, ruined only by hundreds of old European and American obese travelers who come here to take advantage of poor young girls.

- On an island in Thailand I went through a section of jungle (incredibly hard experience to reach a beach otherwise only accessible by boat. At the beach, ready to dive, I see a man from the "Discovery channel" who forbids me to enter the water because he is shooting a documentary... From now on I only watch National Geographic.

- Angkor Wat in Cambodia is definitely the most amazing archaeological site I've ever seen.

- Kuala Lumpur is one of the richest cities in Southeast Asia and consequently an immigration destination for almost all other Asian nations. The integration and respect between all the different ethnic groups is incredible. Muslim women wearing hijiabs, Indians wearing turbans, Europeans in suits and ties, Chinese who spit, Turkish people who smoke, Ceylonese who sell roses... All combined in a spectacular mix.

- The first evening in Bangkok, I arrived at the hostel at 8pm after thirteen hours by bus, and my intention was to go to bed early... however, in the end I returned to the hostel at 5am... The second evening in Bangkok my intention was to party... I have not returned to a hostel.

- In Laos, Cambodia and Thailand, you look at people's faces, you look at their houses and then you understand that money does not bring happiness.

To watch the video *"Crossing Asia by land - From Italy to Indonesia and.... Australia"* about this report, search the link or scan the QR code with your device

www.youtube.com/watch?v=hl0ZcP1u-Bg

FROM SINGAPORE TO MILAN IN HITCHHIKIN

After 139 days spent crossing Asia over land, I decided to fly to Australia to visit the country and find a job to earn back the money I had spent travelling in the last few months. I arrived in Australia at the end of December 2014 with a regular working visa. After the first month (that I spent travelling between Sydney, Melbourne and Adelaide) I decided to settle down in Adelaide, the capital of South Australia, where, besides already knowing a few people, I would have much less competition finding a job. No backpackers would choose Adelaide, a city considered extremely boring compared to the multicultural and dynamic Melbourne and Sydney. For me, however, it was perfect. In just one week I found three jobs that guaranteed me about a thousand dollars per week, a salary that I would never have earnt in Italy. During the day I worked in an appliance company where I fixed ovens and fridges and organized the warehouse. In the evening and often until late at night, I was busy in the cold storage of a food warehouse near home where, with three other guys, I loaded tons of food boxes onto trucks that would distribute the food to shops around the city the next morning. On the weekend as a third job, I took care of a quadruplegic lady, who was suffering from multiple sclerosis, supporting her in her home.

In just one month I was able to regain the money spent during my six months of travel in Europe, Asia and Australia, and even more, I started earning some extra cash. With the bank account growing I decided to slow down a bit and reduce my working hours so I could enjoy more of the Australian lifestyle. Most importantly, reducing my work allowed me to start thinking about making another trip once finishing my year in Australia. I had crossed Asia by land from Milan to Indonesia in my journey coming to Australia, passing through Russia and the North of the Asian continent. Why not return to Milan (once again without taking planes) but passing through the sub-Himalayan regions, through Central Asia and the Middle East? In the winter of 2016, more than a year after I had left home, I decided to return home over land once more... this time using an even less conventional form of "transportation" ... hitch-hiking!

Route Map: Singapore, Malaysia, Thailand, Burma, India, Nepal, India, China, Kazakhstan, Kyrgyzstan, Tajikistan, Uzbekistan, Turkmenistan, Iran, Turkey, Bulgaria, Serbia, Croatia, Slovenia, Italy.

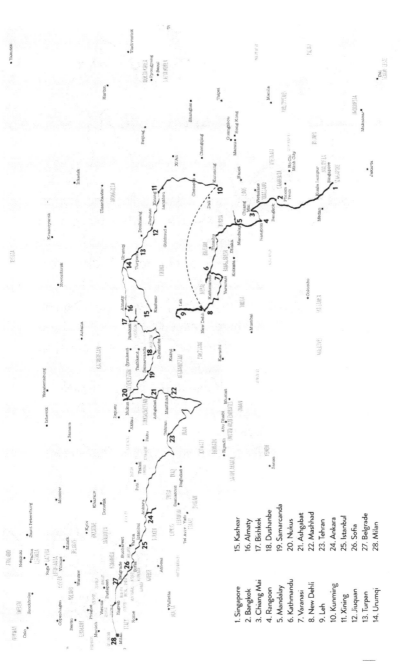

1. Singapore
2. Bangkok
3. Chiang Mai
4. Rangoon
5. Mandalay
6. Kathmandu
7. Varanasi
8. New Delhi
9. Leh
10. Kunming
11. Xining
12. Jiuquan
13. Turpan
14. Urumqi
15. Kashgar
16. Almaty
17. Bishkek
18. Dushanbe
19. Samarcanda
20. Nukus
21. Ashgabat
22. Mashhad
23. Tehran
24. Ankara
25. Istanbul
26. Sofia
27. Belgrade
28. Milan

FIRST REPORT
OF THE RETURN TRIP TO ITALY
HITCHHIKING
MARCH - APRIL 2016

Nations crossed: Singapore, Malaysia, Thailand, Burma

1 night spent in a plastic castle in a children's playground in Singapore

2 minutes, the fastest time it took me to hitch a lift (hitch-hiking in Bagan, Burma)

3 questions that a Muslim man usually asks you when he gives you a lift: "Where are you from?", "Are you married?", "Are you muslim?" ... The third question always made me a bit nervous

4 hours, the longest wait for a lift (50 km north of Kuala Lumpur)

8 kg lost after 40 days of travel

15+ lifts got hitch-hiking between Malaysia, Thailand and Burma

Some gems, especially from Burma:

- In Burma they drive on the right... and the steering wheel is on the right. Overtaking other cars is a survival challenge.

- On April 16th I celebrated the New Year in Burma. In Burma it is the year 1378.

- During the New Year holidays all Burmese public offices, banks and some public transport are usually closed for 10 days. A German tourist even had the courage to tell me "Not even in Naples ..." (an Italian city famous for its laziness).

- Crossing the road in Ulan Bator in Mongolia was the most dangerous experience of my trip so far. Just because I had not yet crossed the roads in Yangon, the capital of Burma. In comparison, Ulan Bator is like Switzerland!

- Bagan, in Burma, is the largest religious site in the world. It contains something like 500 temples scattered around an area of forty miles.

- A week in Burma lasts 8 days. Wednesday is a "double day." Wednesday one commences at midnight and extends until 12pm and Wednesday two goes from 12pm to midnight. Being born on Wednesday afternoon brings bad luck.

- The celebrations of the Burmese New Year last for 4 days and consist exclusively of throwing buckets of water. On the fourth day, the streets of the center of Mandalay city were so flooded that I saw children swimming in the street (no joke, only their head could be seen coming out of the water).

- On the mountains in the north-eastern part of Burma I rented a motorbike to get away from the tourist routes and instead I visited some mountain villages. The idea itself was brilliant, but in the third village I was greeted by a local independence army (SSA). I've never seen so many guns, not even in the movies ...

- It seems that the only way to communicate in the Burmese cities is through using the horn (and it probably is).

- Gasoline is made strictly with the funnel and plastic bottle.

- Because the Leicester football team, coached by the Italian trainer Claudio Ranieri, is leading English Premier league, every Burmese and Thai parson can pronounce (more or less correctly) and remember my name.

- When I crossed the Thai-Burmese border there was so much traffic that for 45 minutes I did not understand which side of the road the bus was supposed to drive on.

- The Burmese girls, although they color cheeks with some yellow spots, are the most beautiful in Southeast Asia... they are not all beautiful, but the beautiful ones are really pretty!

- In Kuala Lumpur I watched a football match at the stadium (I do not know which league). Apart from the obvious low skill level, I was shocked by the fact that at the end of the first half everyone was smoking - referees, coaches and players included.

- When the British settlers arrived in Malaysia there were just a few hundred Chinese people throughout the country. In needing of labor, the British opened Malaysia's doors to Chinese workers. The result 20 years later was a Chinese population of two hundred thousand people.

- The national sport in Thailand is Muay Thai but football-tennis is very popular in the streets. Their skills are phenomenal!

- Driving from Milan to Rome (500km) is definitely faster than going from the suburbs to the center of Bangkok!
- Public swimming pools in Malaysia do not have lanes. You have free choice to swim in vertical or horizontal directions. To be different I started to swim in a circle, like a shark, and nobody complained.

To watch the video *"Crossing Asia by land – Chapter six – Myanmar"* about this report, search the link or scan the QR code with your device.

www.youtube.com/watch?v=ZLoAqZ6fuZE

SECOND REPORT
OF THE RETURN TRIP TO ITALY
APRIL - MAY 2016

Nations crossed: Burma, India (only small states above Bangladesh), Nepal

1 dog that bit my arse in India

16 days of solo trekking on the Himalayan mountains

45 minutes crying after climbing 1000 metres uphill to see Mount Everest... Only to find the sky was too foggy to get a good view.

4773, the highest peak reached (Kyanjin Ri)

8420+ metres of uphill climbing

8460+ metres of downhill climbing

16880+ metres, the total height difference

Some gems from Burma, India and Nepal:

- In Burma instead of smoking, they chew a rolled-up leaf with some kind of walnut and lime mixture. This mix releases a red substance (like blood) in their mouths, which they then spit on the ground. This practice results in roads, walls and car doors covered with blood red patches.

- During New Year's Eve in Burma I saw a fight between two different factions of the Burmese police. With their hands they were not very effective, but with bamboo canes they were phenomenal.

- Buses in India do not generally leave at the scheduled time but leave only when they are completely full. A 'full' bus can include goats, chickens and people on the roof. After the initial delay, several breaks are made to the temples to make offers and color the forehead with a red spot.

- In many villages in India the local "Holy Man" corresponds to the "pusher" and sells drugs.

- The most famous Italian in India is Don Bosco (an Italian Saint). I found several schools dedicated to him.

- In India and Nepal, the scaffolding of the houses under construction are all made with bamboo pipes.

- Buddha was born in Nepal.

- In the city of Guwahati in India, not knowing what to do, I went to see the local youth football team's training sessions. The only thing in common between Indian and European football is that the "fat" child is always the goalkeeper.

- In Nepal I often ate rice in the street which was usually served in newspaper sheets wrapped into a cone. On the Himalayas, having no newspapers, I ate rice wrapped in the math homework of the restaurant owner's son.

- Also, according to the Hindus, the dog is "the man's best friend.". In fact, the dog is considered the last reincarnation before becoming a man.

- Buddhists and Hindus are always relaxed. What they cannot do in this life they will do it in the next one.

- In a camp of Tibetan refugees in India, I played basketball. It's incredible how they never jump at a fake shot. Basically, Bodiroga and Olajuwon could not play successfully in Tibet.

- In Nepal the cost of restaurants and anything else is determined by the altitude of where you buy it. A bottle of water, for example, at 1000m altitude costs 30 rupees, whereas at 2500 m it may costs up to 300 rupees.

- The 1070 metres altitude that I made the first day in 6 hours with a 12 kg backpack and Salomon shoes, a Sherpa (Himalayan ethnic group) makes in 9 hours with 50 kg on his shoulders (50kg!) The shoes he wears? Flip-flops.

- In Nepal, on the slopes of Himalaya, so much marijuana grows, that if the Nepalese began to take care of it, in 10 years they would be able to compete with Colombia.

- In the North-East of India there is a local tribe, the Naga, which stopped eating human meat only a few decades ago.

- A girl in Kathmandu was amazed when I told her that in Italy we speak Italian, in Spain they speak Spanish and French in France... She believed that in Europe we all speak English.

- In Asia there are no barber shops, so I usually went to the hairdresser and borrowed a razor so I could shave my beard myself. This simple process taking about 10 minutes attracted such a big public presence.

- 90% of the villages in the Himalayas are not serviced by roads. All the goods that arrive in the village (food, cigarettes, bottles, clothes, etc.) are carried on the shoulders of the so-called porter (generally from the Sherpa ethnic group). The salary of a porter depends on how many metres of difference in height he travels. Generally, it is about 7/8 € every 1000 metres. Typically, 1000 meters are travelled in 9-10 hours. The weight of the load is usually between 30 and 50 kg and the "backpack," instead of having two braces resting on the shoulders, has only one "brace" resting on the forehead.

- A Sherpa boy asked me which month we have the monsoon season in Italy. When I explained to him that in Italy we do not have the monsoons and rainy season, at first he started laughing thinking that I was joking. When he realised that I was serious, he just said, "Oh man, you're so lucky!"

- The concept of "all you can eat" was born in Nepal. The typical dish called *Dal Bhat* is nothing but rice, a sauce of lentils and fried potatoes/vegetables that are served without stopping until you say you've had enough.

- Nepal is 800 km wide and 200 km long. The border shared with India is about 150 metres above sea level, while the border shared with Tibet is about 7000/8000 metres above sea level. This means that Nepal, only 200 km latitude, has one of the most incredible, vast, differentiated and condensed amounts of flora and fauna on the planet.

- In addition to the incredible variety of flora and fauna in Nepal there is an incredible variety of ethnic groups. In fact, there are more than 70 different castes (ethnic groups with different traditions). Each caste has between 10 and 20 different clans. There are more than 170 different languages spoken. The castes living on the mountains, for example Sherpa and Tamang, are

Buddhist whereas those living in the plains, for example Bramini, are Hindu.

- In the villages in the Himalayas there are no roads, electricity, television, radio, or internet. They do not have books or even drink alcohol. During the day they can only work hard and in the evening, when the cold comes, they sit around the wood stove and chat, laugh and sing. They do not seem less happy than us, Western people.

THIRD REPORT
OF THE RETURN TRIP TO ITALY
JUNE - JULY 2016

Nations crossed: Nepal, India

3 cows that gored me while I was walking quietly on the street

4 Indians fallen from their bike because there were looking at me instead of the road. One even collided with a scooter and got seriously injured

10 days of meditation in a Buddhist monastery in Kathmandu

10.5 hours of daily meditation

23 kg lost since I left Italy, almost two years ago

Some gems from India and Nepal:

- Varanasi is one of the holy cities for Hindu people... I have rarely seen such a magical place.

- In Indian cities I shared the road with millions of mopeds, hundreds of rickshaws but also with monkeys, camels, buffaloes and cows... lots of cows... hundreds of cows!

- To die in the holy city of Varanasi in India is considered a fortune, because dying there allows you to reach nirvana directly. Every day on the banks of the Gange river, that runs through the city, up to 200/300 bodies are burned on the beach. The ashes are then thrown into the river with flowers and ointments. It is incredible to see how just a few dozen metres away there are people taking a bath and washing their clothes ...

- The bodies of children, pregnant women and religious men have the right to be thrown into the Ganges without being cremated. During a short boat ride on the Gange I saw three semi-floating bodies stranded on the bank river and hundreds of children a few metres away washing themselves and playing.

- The Gange near Varanasi reaches a depth of 20 metres (who knows how many bodies are down there!) and a width of about 80m in the dry season and up to 200m during the rainy season.

- The roads in Nepal are so busy that to prevent people from buying more cars (making the roads even busier) the Nepalese government has imposed a tax of 200% on the purchase of a car. The fee is higher if the car is not of Indian production.

- The main Nepalese cities are Kathmandu (the capital) and Pokhara. They are about 250km from one to another which can be travelled in 7-8 hours if there are no accidents. If there are accidents, it may take up to 12 hours to get to one city to the other. I've made the trip three times and there were accidents two of the three times I made the journey.

- I have been in many "poor" or disadvantaged countries, but only in India I have seen true poverty.

- The earthquake in 2016has definitely hit Nepal to a large extent but not just because of the earthquake itself. More problems arose in Nepal when India, after the earthquake, decided to cease trade with Nepal. The reason? Nepal was "guilty" of having accepted economic aid from China.

- The national sport in India is cricket. You can see a lot of children, teenagers and adults playing it in the streets.

Incalculable damages happen every day when playing a sport in which the goal is to hit the ball as hard and as far as possible. By the way... Cricket is not so bad.

- Just outside Kathmandu I had a meditation experience in a Dharma monastery. For ten days I lived without talking to anyone and without anyone talking to me. I lived without books, without my phone, without being able to perform any physical or sexual activity, without eating meat, smoking or drinking alcohol. Ten hours of mediation per day was spreaded between four am in the morning and nine pm. I had never done anything like that before, but it was an incredible experience which I will do again in the future and recommend to everyone.

- In Hindu holy cities like Varanasi or Rishikesh there is no meat in the restaurants, because it is against Hindu tradition. On the other hand, marijuana is legal because the Holy Shiva more than 3000 years ago had the "hobby" of smoking a joint after meals and before sleeping.

- At the Agra train station, I saw a monkey stealing sunglasses from a gentleman and returning it in exchange for a banana.

- The difference between Buddha and Jesus is that Buddha did not perform miracles but rather was much more realistic than Jesus. Instead of raising Lazarus from the dead, Buddha would have explained to the two sisters of the deceased that death is a normal human experience and that it happens to everyone sooner or later.

- The Taj Mahal in the city of Agra is considered one of the seven wonders of the world. It is certainly a fascinating construction, but not as beautiful as the Milan Cathedral!

- I have never believed in saints, witches and other such things, but one night in Delhi as I was walking, an old Sikh man approached me and started saying accurate statements about my life. I stopped and listened to him. He gave me a black and white picture with portraits of about thirty Sikh "holymen" and made me pick one of them. I was skeptical, so I choose the one that looked like Bob Marley most. At that point he wrote something on a piece of paper and put it in my hand, telling me to think of a color. I thought of the colour orange... I opened the little piece of paper and it said "ORANGE." He took another piece of paper, wrote something else and put it in my hand, saying "Think of a number between 1 and 30." I instinctively thought of my age, 28. I opened the paper, it said "28!" I told him "let's find a quiet place to talk man, I want to know more about my future!".

- In Italy, a mango cost between 2 to 3 € each. In India they cost 50 cents per kg. This, in the early days, made my Indian food "Mangocentric". But then I had to surrender to the intestinal war that a kilogram of mangoes a day can create inside your body ...

- In India there are train wagons and subways for women only.

- 50% of Indians are of the Hindu religion. About 20% are Sikh, another 20% are Muslim and the remaining 10% are Buddhist. It is incredible to see the religious integration in the country. Even the Hindus in Varanasi, who are vegetarians, accept that the Muslims butcher and eat meat. Muslims on their side ensure not to offend the Hindus, eating chicken to avoid killing cows and calves, animals sacred to the Hindu people.

- The food at the monastery across my ten day stay consisted of a poor breakfast of a bowl of chickpeas and sweet rice. For lunch I had vegetables and half a kilo of rice and for dinner, half a banana and a bowl of puffed rice. Though there was not much to eat, because I was not moving but instead sitting and meditating, I did not feel hungry.

- During the ten hours of daily meditation there were three hours (one in the morning, one in the early afternoon and one in the late afternoon) when it was "forbidden" to move. Three hours motionless. I have never suffered physically so much in my life... it was the most painful experience I have ever had.

- Many people I met on the trip before entering India told me that you either love it or hate it. I am on team "love it".

To watch the video *"Crossing Asia by land – Chapter Seven – India"* about this report, search the link or scan the QR code with your device.

www.youtube.com/watch?v=GsfDSafJDyU

FOURTH REPORT
OF THE RETURN TRIP TO ITALY
JULY - AUGUST - SEPTEMBER 2016

Nations crossed: India, China, Kazakhstan and Kyrgyzstan

1 knife that a man holds to my throat, asking for my money, in a park in Almaty, Kazakhstan

2 visas that I have been denied, Pakistani and Chinese. I eventually obtained a Chinese visa after a letter from the Italian embassy in Delhi proved that I was just a tourist, not a journalist, soldier or spy

3 days solo travelling the Indian mountains between the regions of Kashmir and Ladakh to escape a civil warfare that was going on right in Kashmir as I entered the region

4 visas that I still need to get to allow me to make my way home: Tajik, Uzbek, Turkmen and Iranian

Some gems from the countries visited:

- In India the cow is a sacred animal so at McDonald's the menu choice is reduced to the McFilet-O-Fish, McChicken and McVeggie burger.

- In the Indian region of Rajasthan, each of the main cities has a specific color. For example, the city of Jaisalmer is all yellow, Jaipur is all pink ...

- The road between the cities of Manali and Leh on the Himalayan mountains in India is one of the most dangerous in the world. Across 200-300 km, it climbs 3 mountain passes over 4000metres in altitude. In some places, even if you do not believe in *God*, you realize that you are praying to someone so that the bus does not veer the road, rolling to the bottom of the valley at least 200-300 metres below.

- On the Himalayas in India for the first time in my life I saw a "halo 22 degrees," a particular optical phenomenon that forms a black and circular spot around the sun.

- A hundred kilometers before reaching the city of Leh in India, the bus travelled the second highest road in the world, sitting 5300 metres altitude. Right on the top there is the classic break for taking photos and using the toilet. Since there is not a real bathroom, I had to walk a fair distance to find a rock upon which I could hide behind to do my business. When the bus sounded the horn, ready to leave, I had just finished and, without remembering that I was at 5300 metres with limited oxygen, I started running towards the bus across those few hundred meters. Upon arriving at the bus I could no longer breathe and seriously thought to die there. At the entrance to each Buddhist temple are painted the "Four Kings", each of them in a different color and from a different cardinal point. Their role is to protect the temple. If I have not misunderstood, the king of the north is blue and holds a sword, while the one from the south is white and plays a mandolin.

- During my trip I was often asked the classic and tricky question about which place I liked the most. I always mentioned Mongolia and some Chinese provinces. However, since visiting Ladakh in India I now have a precise answer. Ladakh with its desertic mountains at 4500 metres altitude and its Tibetan Buddhist temples, is the most beautiful region I have seen in my journey.

- The Indian government has occupied the Kashmir region for several decades with a massive military presence. This is not appreciated by the local inhabitants who would like total independence.

- The genetic mix of the Kashmir population is a mix of Indian, Pakistani, Tibetan and Central Asian ethnic backgrounds and makes the somatic traits of these people incredible. It is not uncommon to see people with dark skin and bright green or blue eyes. Furthermore, the difficult environmental conditions make them look much older than what they really are.

- In India the system of keeping streets clean was very simple until 20-30 years ago. People ate food using leaves as plates and once finishing their meal, threw the garbage on the ground where the next cow passing by would clean it up, eating the leftovers. The advent of plastic has changed this because the cow cannot eat it and therefore plastic stays around without being collected.

- China is growing rapidly, creating a new class of extremely rich young people. I happened to hang out with some eighteen-year-old boys, who were the owners of companies worth 3-4 million dollars.

- I believe that hygiene practices in India and China changing radically and improving. They seemed less dirty than I imagined. In Delhi, for example, I saw more squirrels than mice. The one mouse I did see, however, was as big as my forearm.

- In China I spent several days with a group of Chinese boys and discovered that very often in China is the girl who courts the man. Interestingly, the boys are often way too "picky!" What would happen in Italy if girls courted the boys?

- With the globalization process of people migrating from Western countries and the massive expansion and economic growth of China in all its own provinces, lots of places and ethnic groups are losing their unique characteristic and traditions. In Lhasa, the capital of Tibet, a city on the mountain, they are building new infrastructure and buildings very useful for local people but totally far from the local traditions. In Xinjiang, a Chinese Muslim region, more and more people have started to shave their beards, typical of their culture.

-In Kazakhstan, 20% of girls are from Russian families, with the remaining 80% of Kazakh girls from an Asian background with their physical features softened by the influence of Russian physical characteristics. This guarantees Kazakhstan the gold medal as the country with the prettiest girls I have seen on the journey.

- Xinjiang, western region of China, is populated by Uyghurs, a particular Chinese ethnic group of the Muslim religion. They have particular mosques and mud houses, but the thing that shocked me most was seeing a Chinese person cooking Doner Kebab.

- On radio in Kyrgyzstan, generally after three Russian songs it plays an English song and then an Italian song. Three local songs then one Beatles or Rolling Stones or Pink Floyd song and then a song by Celentano or Albano or Toto Cotugno. Italian singers from the sixties that are no longer popular even in Italy but remain popular in central Asia!

- After 6 months in Southeast Asia, India, Nepal and China, I had forgotten that onion even existed. Biting a sandwich in the street in the capital of Kyrgyzstan and tasting its unmistakable flavor was a mystic experience.

- The most famous Italian in Kazakhstan is Adriano Celentano (my grandma's favorite singer). His face with a rose in his mouth is the advertising image of the local telephone company.

- In the Jammu and Kashmir region in India, roughly 30% of people living there are Buddhist Tibetans, 30% Shiite Muslims and 30% Sunni Muslims. There are no problems among the civil population but there is tension with the Indian government that controls the region. In the Qinghai region in China, all the immigrants (Chinese Han, Tibetan Buddhists and Chinese Muslims) live in peace. In the Xinjiang region (still in China), Chinese Han, Kazakhs, Tajiksis and Muslim Uyghurs live all together peacefully. The only problems are between the Chinese government and the extreme fringes of some Muslim terrorists who entered the region a few years ago. Based on these observations, I think that "normal people" are always willing to live peacefully and in mutual respect, while governments and religions with their territorial, economic and ideological interests undermine the stability of the population.

To watch the video *"World Nomad Games 2016, Cholpan Ata, Kyrgizsthan"* about this report, search the link or scan the QR code with your device.

www.youtube.com/watch?v=WSu2wbyrNYU

FIFTH REPORT
OF THE RETURN TRIP TO ITALY
SEPTEMBER-OCTOBER-NOVEMBER 2016

Nations crossed: Kyrgyzstan, Tajikistan, Uzbekistan, Turkmenistan and Iran

1 attempt made to enter Afghanistan illegally, crossing the river Amu Darya at dusk, which is the border with Tajikistan. The attempt failed (I guess it was better like this)

2 hours spent standing in front of the first police officer at the first passport control station at the Turkmen border. After collecting my passport, he carried on watching his movie.

3 taxi drivers with whom I almost had a fight in Kyrgyzstan... So basically, all the taxi drivers I met...

4 hours spent crossing the Uzbek border. In Uzbekistan it is forbidden to enter with pornographic and/or religious material. At the border police control, before they let me in, a police officer checked all my 6000 travel photos to check if there was any "dirty" material. The process went all smoothly until officer came up with the brilliant idea of checking my WhatsApp groups...

27 the number of nations or tribes participating at the "World Nomad Games" hosted in Cholpon-Ata in Kyrgyzstan

50 Iranians who in less than one month offered me a meal, a cup of tea, a cake or a bed. If alcohol was not prohibited, I would have been drunk every day, I guess. 300 km walked along Afghanistan border, with just a river in between me and Afghanistan.

Some perspectives on the places I visited:
- In August I attended the Olympic games of the nomad people, this year hosted in Kyrgyzstan. They were the same as the Olympic games as we Westerners understand them, but instead of playing soccer, basketball, swimming or athletic competitions the sports are "hawk hunting", "different types of fights," "horse races," "shooting with the bow" and the "Kok Boru".
- Around 27 nations and tribes competed for the various medals at the Nomad Games, which for them carried the same meaning of the medals that were chased at the Rio de Janeiro Olympic Games last summer. Indeed, perhaps the meaning is even more significant as someone competes for "nations" that do not exist on the map and that just through this "international competition" can legitimise their existence.
- The most popular discipline at the World Nomad Games is the "Kok Boru" ... A sort of basketball played on horseback on a field 100-150 meters long where the goal is to put a slaughtered sheep, used as a ball, inside a huge basket!!!
- I'm not a martial arts expert but during the wrestling matches at the Nomad Games, the dislocated elbows

and dislocated shoulders seemed to me to be more accepted than it really should be!

- In Tajikistan I saw the first "Afghan person in Afghanistan" of my life. He was on the other side of the river and when he saw me, wave his hand to greet me. I waved back to him. We were 20 meters away, but never in my life did I feel so different and so far from another human being.

- It took 17 minutes for three Kyrgyz nomads to erect a yurt (their huge tents) suitable to house 8-10 people. I do not think the American Army can do better than that.

- In the mouths of the Central Asian population there is more gold than in the Bank of Italy. It is not clear whether having gold teeth is a necessity or just fashion.

- In 24 days in Kyrgyzstan I saw many more horses than people.

- Hitchhiking in Tajikistan and Kyrgyzstan, I was shocked by the fact that on every single lift I got, we punctured at least one tire.

- At the sacred springs of Bibi Fatima (daughter of Muhammad) on the mountains in Tajikistan, a Tajik boy, there to bath, came out of the water and fainted, violently hitting his head against a rock. All the people around were scared, and nobody helped the guy. I lifted his body (totally naked, like me at that moment) and I took him out in the open fresh air, lying him down and giving him the classic slaps on the face to make him wake up. Just after a minute, the boy, still unconscious, began to scream and start kicking and punching the air. I tried to calm him without causing any further concussions. After another 5 minutes of delirium with him unconscious and shouting, I ask the only Tajik man who speaks English, a friend of the injured guy, to call a doctor immediately. He told me not to worry because we were in a holy place and his friend was probably having sacred visions or talking with *God*.

- In Tajikistan, the people are all very kind, except the police. The level of corruption within the police force is crazy. In the last lift I received, which lasted about six hours, the driver of the vehicle with whom I was traveling was stopped at least 15 times by several policemen for "ID control". The only way to avoid the control is to give the classic bribe. On the fifteenth time we were stopped in a day, the driver was totally depressed and I was so frustrated that I could not control a "Fuck off," a little bit too loud towards the young policeman.... And... Passport control and fine dropped to me.

- If you have a dirty car in Tajikistan and you are stopped by the police, the bribe is not enough. You get a proper fine!

- In the last 3 months of travel I saw many nations with "regimes" or "dictators." The "dictator" of the Republic of Tajikistan is certainly the nicest. He began as the dictator 20-25 years ago (practically since the birth of Tajikistan itself) with 93% of the public votes and his big face is everywhere! If you walk near a workshop there is a photo of him repairing cars in a suit and tie without sweating or getting dirty. If you pass near a farm there is a picture of him plowing the fields, always in a jacket and tie and always without sweating. How can you not love him?

- In the eastern part of Uzbekistan, I went to visit the remains of Lake Aral. Until 1960, the lake covered an area of about 70 thousand square kilometers (approximately as big as the North of Italy) and guaranteed one hundred thousand tons of fish per year. Then the Soviet Union decided that Uzbekistan had to become the province that cultivated cotton, so all the tributaries of Lake Aral were diverted to irrigate the new cotton fields. Almost sixty years later, Uzbekistan is the world's third largest cotton producer. While Lake Aral is a huge desert wasteland and all the families in the area that lived thanks to the fishing industry now live in total poverty.

- After three months in Central Asia I re-evaluated the figure of Gorbachev. Dismantling the Soviet Union has in fact given independence to nations which their independence did not interest to, creating a series of new non self-sustainable nations What did Uzbekistan do with all that cotton if the textile industries were then in Russia? Or how did Tajikistan, mainly mountainous, get certain fruits or vegetables if they had to be imported from another country?

- In Tajikistan, women always sit in the back seats of a car.

- In about 1970 the Soviet Union, searching for oil in the Turkmenistan desert, accidentally caused a huge chasm above a "gaseous deposit" causing the uncontrolled outflow of gas. The only way to limit environmental damage was to burn it. For the last forty years in the

Turkmen desert there has been a huge crater with a permanent fire.

- Turkmenistan certainly has the most repressive dictatorial regime of all the Central Asian republics. The pictures and statues of the current dictator are everywhere! In Ashgabat, the capital, there is literally a policeman every 50 meters.

- At least 50% of women in Iran have cosmetic surgery on their nose.

- Some common shampoo fragrances in Uzbekistan are garlic and egg.

- The Iranian people, thanks to the cornerstones of Islam which "consecrates" the concept of hospitality, are the most hospitable people I have ever met. One day, for example, I was walking on the outskirts of the city of Isfahan and I met a worker on his lunch break wearing stained work overalls holding an inviting dish of rice in his hands. He was clearly a mechanic and that was his meal. I was starving, looking at that plate of rice in his hands. He understood that I was hungry and without speaking English took me into his workshop and offered me his lunch. All my refusal and attempts to divide the portion equally were refused. That day Abdullah skipped his lunch to make me eat.

- The "mess" that *Alexander the Great* made between Turkey, Iran and parts of southern Tajikistan makes no sense.

- The Iranians are very kind, except in the car when they are willing to kill you rather than let you cross the road first.

- In Iran there is an absolute obligation for all women to cover their heads with the hijab. Older women wear it proudly, covering their whole head. The younger ones try to cover the smallest possible portion to let their hair be more visible. It may seem stupid but walking as a tourist through the crowded streets next to women all wearing the hijab is not an easy experience. The hijab limits a woman's peripheral vision and does not allow others to understand their directions.

- On public transport in Iran the men sit in front the rows so they cannot see the women sitting in the back rows.

- In some Iranian cities, at the entrance door there are two different bells, one for men and the other for women, so that the residents know whether the husband or wife should go to open the door.

- The Kurds are the largest ethnic group without their own nation. Twenty million people are scattered between Turkey, Iran, Iraq and Syria. The Kurds wear very wide trousers and they are even kinder, if possible, than the Iranians.

- The Iranian revolution by Ayatollah Khomeini and the massive return to Islamic customs has several implications, some positive and others negative. It has reinforced a "nationalist" feeling and the love for their culture has slowed down the globalization process (fortunately) and has preserved Iran from a possible territorial disintegration - probably desired by some Western countries - similar to the one that happened in the former Yugoslavia.

- For 28 days in Iran I did not see the hair of any woman. I almost forgot how beautiful women's hair can be. On one of my last days in the country, a German lady at my hostel forgot to cover her head and came out of her room showing her long blonde hair. I thought I was about to faint.

- Many Iranians I met asked me to tell people, once I was back in Italy, that even if they are Muslim and in many Western countries, we just see them as terrorists, they are just good people with no interest in religious wars or desire to attacks. I wish to start spreading this message here: The Iranians, people of Islamic religion, are the kindest, most charitable and most willing to help people I've ever met in my life.

To watch the video *"Crossing Asia by land – Chapter eight - Central Asia"* about this report, search the link or scan the QR code with your device.

www.youtube.com/watch?v=APmyvy6pH4Y

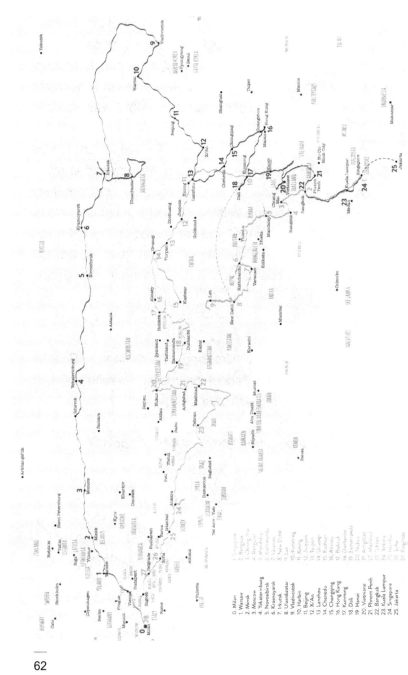

WORKING AS A PHYSICAL EDUCATION TEACHER IN CHINA

It took me ten months to cross Asia from Singapore to Italy by hitch-hiking. I finally returned to Milan in December 2016 after more than 800 days travelling through Europe, Asia and Oceania. I felt better than ever, filled with the joy of being home again after such a long time and excitement from the incredible adventure that had just ended. I had been able also to complete the return journey with a very small daily budget which allowed me to retain some of the money I had saved from working in Australia. I basically returned home after two years of travel, not only having had sensational experiences, but also with a lot more money than when I had left Italy two years earlier in the summer of 2014.

This situation, combined with a desire to travel not yet completely satisfied, made me consider the possibility of moving abroad once again to work so I could save the money necessary to allow me to do another long trip. I had discovered how easy it was to save money in certain countries and how cheap it was to travel in others. I just had to find a country where I could earn well without spending much. I could have therefore returned to Australia, or I could have tried the working holiday visa in Canada or New Zealand, but in my heart, I felt I wanted to return to Asia and I knew that China would be the perfect place. A country advantageous economically and strategically well placed to visit nations and regions that I wanted to see badly: Sri Lanka, Taiwan and Tibet. In addition, basketball is the most practiced sport in the country, and I would be able to use my degree in physical education and my basketball trainer license to find a job as a teacher. Certainly, a much more interesting option than picking fruit on some Australian farm. Only a few months after returning home I had already started looking for a job abroad... in China.

On 31st August 2017 with a one-way ticket I left home for Shenzhen, a city in the province of Guangdong in southern China. What waiting for me was a year contract as a basketball teacher in a public Chinese primary school. It's impossible not to keep writing about such a "colorful" experience.

SOME BRIEF CONSIDERATIONS ON SHENZHEN AND "EXPAT" LIFE IN CHINA

- Shenzhen, as we understand it, was founded in 1978. So basically, it has the same age of Kobe Bryant, Gianluigi Buffon and Katie Holmes.

- In 1978 there were 30,000 people in Shenzhen, mainly fishermen and traders. In 2017 there are 13 million, taking the title for the most rapid population increase in the planet. Thirty years ago, Shenzhen had the same number of inhabitants of a small Italian town and now it has the same number of inhabitants as London, Paris and Rome collectively.

- Located in the city centre there are clubs and discos designed to attract as many Western customers as possible (which subsequently attracts more Chinese customers). These clubs offer special entrance packages such as "entrance eight euro - All you can drink". That means you pay eight euros to get in and the waitress puts on your table a bottle of vodka, one bottle of rum, one bottle of gin, a dozen cans of soft drinks and a two-litre beer tube ...

- Guangdong, the province where I live, is as big as the whole central and northern part of Italy but it's home to 120 million people (including Hong Kong) which is the same number of inhabitants in Italy and France combined.

- Bao'An, the neighborhood where I live, has a surface area three times bigger than Milan and it is considered the "Bronx" of Shenzhen.

- The Shenzhen Metro has 8 lines, 199 metro stations and over 280 km covered. A trip costs as little as 20 eurocents for a short journey up to a 1.5 euro to cross the city. Line 11, which goes to the airport located 35 km from the city center, has trains traveling at 120 km/h, reaching the airport in just thirty minutes from the city center!

- The "Futian" subway station has 32 exits. Thirty-two!!!

- The number of Western expats in Shenzhen is pretty big. There are significantly more women than men. The most represented nations are Russia and Ukraine.

- Every morning I walk to my school. I walk for eight minutes through the narrow streets of my neighborhood. On my second day of work, I saw a butcher's shop near my school. It exposed photos of the animals on sale and I took a look. There was a goat, a cow and... a dog! I look at the butcher, shocked, who smiles at me and starts barking to confirm that I understood... He sells dogs!!!

- A pint of beer in the city centre costs € 4.50. In bars near my house in the suburbs it costs from sixty to eighty eurocents.

- Five hundred euro is my average monthly expense. It includes renting the apartment, bills, telephone, 30 breakfasts on the street, 30 dinners at the restaurant, a massage session, a few beers on weekends and... 60 soluble coffee Nescafe. I've never missed Italian espresso so much!

- I regularly went to the park to do some physical exercise at the bar and at the parallels after school. Every time, some Chinese locals would ask to take a picture with me. One Sunday morning I was training and after ten consecutive pull-ups, a group of elderly Chinese approached and asked me to pose with them showing my biceps. I felt a bit like Stallone acting Rocky and I posed with virile pride. But then, they started to train themselves... One of them started walking on his hands, two started a complete split contest and another one stood vertically on the parallels, all laughing and chatting... From that moment I started going to the park just to run.

- Body massages are a serious matter here. With twenty euro a tiny little Chinese girl has been able to make all my vertebrae creak using only one hand. With five euro she even cleaned my ears using a toothpick twenty centimeters long... I was afraid that she wanted to get the toothpick out of the other ear!

- Unlike Italians, when Chinese children play "guards and thieves" they prefer to be guards. At first I was intrigued by their attitude. Thinking about it, maybe only in Italy we prefer to be thieves compared to the nobler role of the guard.

- It has been a weird experience to see my colleagues' dormitory. Fifteen male teachers and fifteen female teachers live there, all in their twenties, all single. It has been weird to see that they all go to sleep at ten o'clock in the evening without leaving traces of beer cans or condom papers. In Italy a place like that would become a party paradise!

- It is very common to see a Western man dating a Chinese girl. It is almost impossible to see a Western girl dating a

Chinese man. This situation has created a disproportion in the sexual activity of Western immigrants in Shenzhen where men have no competition, being able to choose from both Chinese and foreign girls, while Western women can find only find Western men. Of course, this is made more challenging due to having to compete with the Chinese women. I saw Russian ladies who in Italy would have men lining up for them complaining that no one is inviting them for a drink.

- In Shenzhen there are three types of taxis: the red ones, which can run all over the city, the green ones, which can only run in a specific neighborhood and the motor-taxi, which are the cheapest and the fastest because they can drive in any street, avenue and highway, even in the opposite direction.

-The supermarkets close at 11.00 pm... The subway closes at 11.30 pm... The hairdressers never close.

To watch the video *"My Chinese apartment... Expat life"* about this report, search the link or scan the QR code with your device.

www.youtube.com/watch?v=1hcQyNaq67E

THE CHINESE PUBLIC SCHOOL
I WORKED

1 the number of foreigner teachers in my school: myself

2 medical figures in the school: the doctor and the nurse

10 policemen

18 English teachers

20 volunteering mothers working at school, checking the order in the corridors, on the stairs and the school exit

30 janitors, caretakers, gardeners, waiters and cooks

46 teachers enrolled in the communist party. Any school must have some.

131 the total amount of teachers in the school

2000+ school students

Some considerations:

- All primary schools in Shenzhen have the same uniform for their students. A blue and white shirt with a small green logo on the chest with "Shenzhen" printed on it. They must also wear a red scarf on Mondays, which gives them a "proletarian communism" touch.

- All children, every day of the week except Wednesday, must wear the school uniform combined with white shoes. On Wednesdays, according to school rules, they are free to decide what to wear. This made me witness of some of worst colour combinations that a human being can choose.

- I share my office with Chinese English teachers. Six lovely girls. It took me a month to learn their names. After six months I still do not know how to pronounce them correctly. They sound like: Siii Uuu, Siii Arr, Siii Fuu, Liu Siii, Lonh and Mou.

- On one of the first days we spent together, my assistant coach told me that he preferred his family than his work. Then he told me not to tell this to anyone.

- I knew that in China burping in public is not considered rude, but to hear my colleagues at school, pretty and tiny twenty-year-old schoolteachers, who burp louder than my uncle at a beer festival. I just couldn't get used to it.

- The math teacher once asked me if the "school gossip", that I drink coffee every morning, was true. "Of course" I told her and I tried to shock her even further, telling her that I even drink one after lunch. She looked at me like I was a cocaine addict.

- On one of the famous Wednesdays where children were free to wear anything they like, a child came to school with a shirt with this message wrote on the chest: "Hang the pedophiles and rapists".

- There is only one English textbook in the province of Guangdong for primary schools. ALL Chinese from 5 to 20 years can say only what is written in that book. When I ask someone "How are you?", everyone (but I mean everyone in any situation, at any time of day, anywhere) answer "Iamfinethankyou!!!" pronounced without dividing pauses.

- For a month I was walking around the school with a package of lollies in my pocket, strawberry Alpenliebe, ready to give it to the first child who answered me in a different way than "Iamfinethankyou!" After a couple of weeks, with the arrival of the first cold, a child answered me saying "I am cold!". In a mixture of amazement and emotion, I gave him the lollies and I thanked him. He took it, looking at me like "This white man with the beard must be bloody crazy!"

- Each class is made up of between forty and fifty pupils.
- If I think about all the sports equipment, I had available to me in the six/seven primary schools where I worked in Italy, it is not even half of what I had available to me in China.
- The children at school are mostly thin, but those who are overweight are really huge...
- Every child with a shaved head reminds me of the movie "The Little Buddha".
- During the rainy days, the physical education classes are automatically cancelled and the students stay in the classroom to read or do their homework.
- While in Italy the "fat" student is generally teased by other kids, in China the "fat" one is "the bully".
- The Chinese classrooms are so crowded that my colleagues teach with a small microphone hanging from their ear to their mouth, projecting their croaking voice from a small box hanging from their skirt.
- During the sunny days all my colleagues used an umbrella while walking in the sun even to walk to the canteen, which was just fifty metes away from school. None likes to have darker skin in China. A math teacher told me once that physical education teachers like me

are very unlucky because when we work outdoors we get darker skin.

- In the end, I realised that children are almost all the same all over the world. There is the "nerdy" child with glasses, the "clumsy" fat child, the shy girl and the rogue dwarf. The homework does not please anyone, changing class is a real noisy mess and a ball can give them happiness.

To watch the video *"My Chinese basketball lessons"* about this report, search the link or scan the QR code with your device.

www.youtube.com/watch?v=eqa1rJWl2p4

SOME CONSIDERATIONS AND ANECDOTES ABOUT CHINA

- In China everyone can decide their own name in English. The accountant of the agency I work for decided to call herself Bella. The funny thing is that her surname is Lì. On the tenth of every month I received a transfer from "Bella Lì", which in Italian means "So cool"!

- In the city of Shenzhen, with its fourteen million inhabitants, the government issued a law to prevent too many people from buy a car and clogging all the city roads. The law states that before buying a car, a person has to buy a license plate. The price for a license plate ranges from five to ten thousand euros, depending on the number combination of the license plate itself. Plates with the number 8 or 6, Chinese lucky numbers, can triple in cost. Alternatively, if you cannot buy the license plate, you can apply to the government lottery and try to get one for free however this generally may take years of waiting...

- In the street restaurants in China, since the dishes cannot be washed, the food is served on dishes wrapped in plastic bags. This means that when the meal is finished the waiter just removes the plastic bag from the plate to reveal the clean plate underneath.

- In Chinese fast food restaurants, the customers don't need to make the effort to go to the bathroom to wash their hands because the meal is served with disposable plastic gloves, so that they can eat without touching the food.

- The consumption of plastic in China is shameful!!!

- On "Women's Day", all female teachers are allowed, by law, to work only half a day. So, in my school where out of 130 teachers, just 15 are male, on the Women's day there were just ten teachers taking care of 2,000 students. Five of my male colleagues pretended to be sick that day and took a day off...

- The "selfie fashion" in China is really exaggerated... Many people put so many filters on their photos that they become unrecognizable, more like a cartoon than a human being.

- It seems that in China people can control the gender of newborns. In my school, each class was comprised of 60-70% boys and just thirty-forty percent girls. I wonder what kind of problems will come when this generation reaches puberty.

- Four is the unlucky number in China because the word has same sound as the word "death." In many buildings the number four is not used and therefore the fourth and fourteenth floors are replaced by 3A or 13A.

- It's pretty common that English sentences appear on Chinese product packages to get more appeal. I saw the worst translations ever in my staying in China. I once bought a snack called "Shit Sugar".

- The amount of food wasted in China is depressing. At my school's canteen, for example, almost all my colleagues filled the tray with as much food as possible and then ate only half of what was on their tray.

- For the weekend of May 1st, I went to the world famous *"UNESCO heritage"* town of Yangshuo in Guangxi. I rented a motorbike to get around freely in the mountains. At lunch time, I found a restaurant by a little pond that served the typical dish of the area, rice and chicken cooked in bamboo stick. Strangely enough, it costs 160 yuan (about twenty euros), but I ordered anyway. After I had ordered, the cook came out of the kitchen to call me and took me to the back yard of the restaurant where there was a big garden full of chickens. Using his cell phone, he translated his message and I read "Which chicken do you want?" Pretty shocked, I picked the biggest one. Half an hour later, after terrible noises from the kitchen, I got a "fresh" chicken in a bamboo stick ...

- Walking in China, even in the big cities, gives you the chance to see so many different animals - hens, geese, dogs on the spit. However, I never expected to see a sturgeon fish of a metre and a half in the street.

- Besides teaching, in China it is easy to find small jobs to get some extra money, especially if you have a beard, long hair and light eyes. The easiest jobs to find are modelling jobs for products to sell on the internet or "the monkey that speaks English". For several months, every week-end I travelled two days out of town to a kind of camp where I was paid to play games, dance and chat with Chinese adults who paid quite a lot of money to partake in this full English immersion.

- The only thing that my little students knew about Italy was "*spaghetti*". Several of my students (but also some of my colleagues) to make fun of me call me "Idaly Mien Laoshi", literally "Spaghetti-Teacher".

- A colleague of mine took me to visit his university in Guangzhou city, the fourth most populated city in China. Students can sleep at the university campus in bedrooms for twelve people, each of them equipped with one bathroom, one shower and one sink. I guess in the morning between the first student to pee and the last one to brush their teeth there must be at least two hours difference.

- The streets in Shenzhen are like the jungle, and, like the jungle there is a precise "food chain". At the base there is the pedestrian, which being the weakest has no rights. None respects him, even on the pedestrian crossing and even if he crosses with the green light he must be careful not to be knocked down. Then bicycles and electric scooters come next, which have the "skill" to drive in the opposite direction and are stronger than pedestrians but can do nothing against the cars. Cars themselves are "eaten" by trucks and buses, authentic "kings of traffic". Because the buses and trucks are the biggest, they can cross roads even on a red traffic light, without respecting any rule. The incredible thing is that everyone lives with extreme acceptance that the biggest vehicle has more rights. I saw pedestrians crossing the road during a green traffic light and not complaining about scooters or cars that, crossing with red traffic light or in the wrong direction, were almost knocking them down.

- When the typhoons arrive, usually around June and July, the schools remain closed.

- Every Chinese has a picture of his face and his fingerprints registered in all government offices. Even for a simple bank levy, you can be photographed. Recently, cameras have been installed at the traffic lights, taking pictures of those pedestrians who cross on a red light. The incredible thing is that the photos are compared with those stored in the government offices to send the fine home.

- Chinese society is very complex and full of contradictions. It is very difficult to understand even when you live there, and it is impossible to know it properly if you have not lived there. It is often criticized for the policy of control, the "non-democracy" but people live really well there. Prosperity is well distributed (in the cities). They do not have the opportunity to vote but they don't really care because they have a government that satisfies them. The unemployment rate is very low and they are conquering the world on an economic level without having ever bombed anyone.

FROM TIBET TO ITALY BY BICYCLE

Living in China was a rich experience which satisfied me beyond my expectations. I was assigned to a school in Shajing District, on the northern outskirts of the suburban Bao'An district. This district is typically unpopular with Western expats because it's forty-five kilometers far from the center and almost uninhabited by other expats. But for me it was the best! I was one of the few "white people" in the district and the only foreign teacher in my school. This allowed me to integrate myself deeply and discover more things around me. The shopkeepers of the neighborhood, at first frightened by my presence, became "friends", sharing with me moments of everyday life without even really being able to communicate. School colleagues became real friends with whom I played basketball or football after school classes. In the district itself, so chaotic, dirty and disorganized, I found peaceful spaces, pedaling every day in the city parks or along the *Pearl River.*

Work at school was fantastic too. Teaching basketball in English, for an Italian native speaker, to classes of fifty Chinese students that did not understand a single word of what I said, was a big challenge that enriched my work skills.

After settling into Chinese life, I started looking for some small jobs to increase the already good teacher's salary. I started working on weekends as an English teacher in a campus outside the city, and I did several photoshoots for a sports backpacks brand that sells their products on *Amazon* and needed a "western model" to promote them. My bank account, as had already happened in Australia, began to grow, allowing me to see the possibility of another period without working and consequently another long trip.

As soon as I moved to China, I already knew that once my work contract expired I would return to Italy overland. But I hadn't yet decided the route or method of transport. I wanted something different than hitchhiking and using public transport, both used in previous trips. I wanted to try something even more adventurous and that would make me as autonomous as possible. I wanted to try something like motorbiking or cycling. In addition, after spending the last three years of my life in Asia, I felt the need to give something back to this wonderful land and its people. I decided to launch a fundraiser, through Facebook, connected to my journey that could help some organizations operating in the area. Cycling from China to Italy felt sufficiently difficult to justify fundraising linked to the journey.

I started looking for an organization to "sponsor" on the Facebook page linked to my trip, *Vagabondiario*, where I invited the people who were following my trip to make a small donation. I immediately found the Tashi Orphan School, thanks to some contacts I had in in India and Nepal. The Tashi Orphan School seemed perfect because in addition to helping children in need and preserving the Tibetan culture, it is managed by local staff, teachers and educators who "know what they are doing". During my travels I came across various non-profit organisations from Western countries who, without realising it, were distorting and changing the culture and habits of the people they were trying to help. In addition, the Tashi Orphan School was funded by a non-profit association based in Italy to which the donations could be made directly, meaning I did not have to collect the money myself and send it to the orphanage.

Once the organisation was identified and the transport was decided, I just had to decide the route. I would leave from Tibet, because visiting Lhasa, the capital of the region, has always been a dream of mine, and because it would give a real connection between the trip and the fundraising. In mid-July 2017 I left for Tibet, leaving my small apartment in Shenzhen. I could not start the trip by bike from Tibet, so my bicycle was waiting for me just outside the northern border of the region.

On July 31, 2018, I got my bicycle, called Princess Wencheng, in the town of Golmud and I began to cycle on the Tibetan plateau to the northwest, towards home, towards Italy.

Route Map: China, Kazakhstan, Uzbekistan, Kazakhstan, Caspian Sea, Azerbaijan, Georgia, Black Sea, Bulgaria, Serbia, Croatia, Slovenia, Italy.

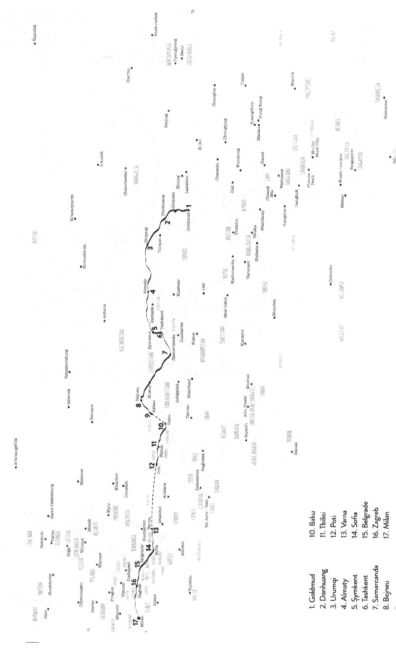

1. Golmud
2. Donhuang
3. Urumqi
4. Almaty
5. Symkent
6. Tashkent
7. Samarcanda
8. Bejneu

10. Baku
11. Tbilisi
12. Poti
13. Varna
14. Sofia
15. Belgrade
16. Zagreb
17. Milan

THE BIRTH OF A DREAM

Out of all the places I wanted to see in the world, the *Potala Palace* in Lhasa, the capital of Tibet and the historic residence of the Dalai Lama, has always been the top! I was a primary school kid when my dad came home with a book. He is a taxi driver and he got the book by collecting points from Esso petrol stations. He could have chosen the cookware set, the Panasonic Walkman or the jacket, but he chose the DeAgostini book titled *"Atlas of Legendary Places"*. The pages smelled like mould, and I can only guess that the gas station owner had kept it in some dark and humid storage room in the last few months, convinced that no one would ever ask for that book. The book talked about sacred places, magical and mysterious buildings, lighting in me, a little child, charm and curiosity, but above all, the deep desire to see all those places upon growing up. I have been lucky, I have already seen many of them- St. Peter's Cathedral in Rome, the Alhambra in Spain, the Meteors in Greece, Samarkand, the Round Table, Ayers Rock and many others. But Tibet, the place that fascinated me most after reading Siddhartha and seeing countless films, seemed so far away, somewhere on the Himalayas mountain ranges. And instead, as is always the case in life, just like a musty book preferred to a jacket, I had been brought here. Today I'm happy, tomorrow who knows? But I realised how important it is, in a world that is beginning to see the danger in "difference", to fascinate children, nurturing their curiosity and the desire to discover.

FIRST REPORT OF THE BIKE TRIP
PLUS WEEK IN TIBET
JULY - AUGUST 2018

Nations crossed: China (Tibet, Qinghai, Gansu, Xinjiang) and Kazakhstan

1 occasion of being arrested by Chinese police just north of Urumqui (no one spoke English, so I have not really figured out what happened)

2 the number of spokes of the back wheel broken

4 flat tires

5 creatures from which I had to escape (shepherd dogs, wild camels, Chinese policemen, mints and a Kazakh boy, who seems to like me a bit too much)

11-13 km/h the average speed uphill or when I have wind against me

18 km/h the global average daily speed

25 km/h the average speed when I listen to AC/DC

30+ people who offered me water, cigarettes, slices of watermelon and even car lifts (which I had to refuse)

42 degrees Celsius the highest temperature I cycled in

100+ policemen who checked my passport in the Chinese region of Xinjiang (two of them even spoke an elementary English)

-120 metres below sea level, the lowest point crossed

156 km the longest distance traveled in a day (from the 122nd km I had the police chasing me)
2374 total km travelled so far
3699 the height of the highest peak reached with the bike

Some considerations and episodes

- On the train to Lhasa, the capital of Tibet, you begin to understand that you have exceeded 3000 metres altitude when you start to have a slight headache and all the children around you start vomiting.
- When climbing mountains above 3000 metres with the bicycle, because of the pressure all of my sealed food bags swelled up almost to the point of explosion and my bicycle wheels were as hard as marble.
- While I was cycling in the desert in the Xinjiang province, I heard two little explosions in my bicycle bag, without understanding where they came from. It was so hot that the lighters I used to start my alcohol oven had exploded, forcing me to have a dinner of raw spaghetti in the evening.
- The Potala Palace in Lhasa, the former residence of the Dalai Lama, is sensational. The complexity and richness of the details make it one of the best buildings I have ever seen in my life. It contains hundreds of rooms connected by narrow tunnels, lavish corridors or small hidden courtyards. Thousands of Buddha statues and its reincarnations are presented. Everything so beautiful that even the Chinese army during the "cultural revolution" in which they destroyed almost all the religious buildings couldn't touch it.

- In a small Kazakh country village, a guy, clearly homosexual, approached me and asked me to take a selfie. I gladly accepted, but when I started pedaling to my next destination he started following me on his bike and as soon as we left the village, he started yelling "pasjhausta" , which means "I beg you", pointing the thick vegetation on the side of the road with the intention to hide there and "enjoy the moment with me". After ten minutes of non-stop supplications I decided to accelerate and run away from him but, being already at the eightieth kilometre of the day and with my bike loaded it took me 10 km and the help of the AC/DC to get rid of him. In Kazakhstan, as in many former Soviet countries, especially in small and remote villages, homosexuality is unfortunately still a very delicate subject. I guess the guy chased me because, as a foreigner, I was his only "chance".

- Road traffic in China is ruled by the law of the biggest. I forgot about it the first day of my cycling adventure when, despite the green light at the traffic light, I was hit by a three-wheeled motorbike that crossed the road on a red light and destroyed my rear wheel.

- Tibetan Buddhism is completely different to the Southeast Asian one. A Tibetan Buddhist monk is a lifetime monk, from the day he enters the monastery until his death. With "Chineseisation" and "globalisation", fewer and fewer young people decide to become monks. Only poor nomadic families are the last to send their children to the monasteries.

- In the steppe in Kazakhstan I found a kind of abandoned tank not far from the road. The sun was almost setting, so I decided to take my last break before pitching my tent a few kilometres later. From the scrap came out a hunter with rifle in his hand who, seeing me on a bike, offered me two apples, water and some sweets. I told him that I was going to sleep in my tent during the night and he smiled at me saying "Watch out for wolves, snakes and scorpions. I've definitely spent quieter nights.

- In Urumqi I took a day off after weeks of cycling in the desert. I decided to go to a swimming pool, to relax a little. The admission fee was 20 yuan + 5 yuan for a mandatory medical examination with the "doctor" who checked if I had any skin diseases.

- I arrived in Almaty in Kazakhstan after a month almost like a hermit between mountains and deserts and I decided to have some fun. So, with some people I had met at the hostel (also Kazakhs), we went out to the clubs in one of those classic evenings when you say to yourself "yes, a couple of beers and we will come back" but then you come home at five am. Towards the closing of the last pub, while all the people were outside to smoke or in the bathroom before leaving, I find myself sitting at the table alone with a girl I had just met and with whom I start talking. She asks me about the bike trip and tells me about her problems with a slightly violent ex-husband. A short while later a huge guy comes along who tells me something extremely aggressive in Kazakh. I think he is a waiter who is telling us that the pub closes soon but, I don't understand this unjustified aggressiveness. I smile to him and I give him a pat and I say, laughing "man take it easy, we leave soon!". He then tells me "I am girl's husband", pointing to the lady I was talking with, grabbing the girl and dragging her away. My first thought is that if I try to stop him, he will smash me but the second thought is for the poor girl, so I get up and try to calm him down. One of the "henchmen" of the violent husband stops me and, very polite and relaxed, tells me "Do not mess up with my brother, he is crazy, we control him!" The poor girl comes back half an hour later, on the way home, in tears.

- I arrived in an emergency situation in Urumqi with two broken spokes of my bike. I stopped at the first cyclist shop to repair them. The mechanic was deaf and could not speak. I found no difference communicating with him compared to almost any other Chinese person.

- Many people ask me where I wash myself when I cycle in remote areas. Well honestly, I do not wash myself. If I have enough water, I refresh my armpits and my face. Yes, entering into my tent is not always pleasant, but fortunately the feet are the part of the body that is farthest from the nose.

- While I was in Lhasa the *Fifa World Cup* was going on, so one night I snuck out of the hotel looking for a place to watch the game. I found a crowded place. The level of "toughness" of the Tibetan youth is sensational, one guy even entered the pub riding his motorbike! But they all smiles and were very generous. People even came to offer me bottles of beer.

- The desert is so dry that when I pedaled and sweated, I always found the arms of the shirt full of salt, a lot of salt...

- One evening in China, in the mountains of Tien Shan, two thousand meters above sea level, after finishing dinner I saw a storm approaching my camp spot. It was a huge one with lightning every five seconds and thunder without interruption... not a nice thing if your bike and the poles of your tent are the only pieces of metal within a radius of 100km. In order not to be hit, I parked the bike as far as possible from the tent and I hid myself in the sleeping bag, praying that the storm would not hit me. After a while it went away, leaving me victim of just a strong wind and just four drops of water. The next day I reached a motorway service, opened the Wi-Fi and read the most famous Italian newspaper website. There was an article about a boy seriously injured by lightning while he was on the beach in South Italy. Who would ever expect to be struck by lightning at the beach? In South Italy for more! I think that life is a series of coincidences... coincidences that we cannot control. For this reason, it is really worth trying to live to the maximum, everyone in his own way, always without saving energy or being frightened.

SECOND TRIP REPORT
SEPTEMBER - OCTOBER 2018

Nations crossed: Kazakhstan and Uzbekistan

0 flat tires (since I've changed it in Urumqi)

2 families who, seeing me pitching my tent, decided to host me at their home

4 consecutive days without showering

6+ liters of water consumed every day in the desert

10+ truck drivers who stopped to give me water

50+ cans of coke drunk

140 avarage kilometers cycled for eight consecutive days to leave the Karakalpakstan desert and the Kazakh steppe as soon as possible

169 the maximum number of kilometers cycled in one day

- At the first village I reached in Kazakhstan an old man, sitting on the roadside and seeing me pass, made me the gesture of drinking from a bottle. I believed he wanted to offer me some water, so I stopped in front of him, but from his jacket he took out a bowl of vodka, insisting that I drink it. The next twenty kilometers I was pedalling talking to wild horses and eagles.

- In Almaty I chatted with the owner of the hostel. I asked her about the Kazakh political situation and she told me that it is excellent because, unlike the other Central Asia states, there is no dictatorship. The president has been in charge for "only" 27 years (basically, since Kazakistan was born) with 98% of the votes!

- A hundred kilometers before Samarkand, the most famous city on the silk road, a farmer, seeing me pitching my tent, invited me to sleep in his little house. The conversation began with the classic question "Atkuda?" - Where are you from? As soon as I answered "Italy," the man exclaimed "Ah Italy...London!". During dinner, as an Italian, I was asked to sing with the old farmer, who quoted all the Italian singers he knows Adriano Celentano, Toto Cutugno and Michael Jackson! Even his wife looked at him weirdly and tried to convince him that Michael Jackson is not Italian, but he remained set on his idea. So, when I was called into the discussion to avoid disappointing him, I lied shamelessly "Michael Jackson? Oh yes, he is from Rome!".

- With all the golden teeth in the Uzbek and Kazakh dentures, Italy could pay off their public debt.

- In Europe we have flocks of swallows and pigeons. In Kazakhstan, outside some cities, I saw flocks of eagles, and considering that they eat rodents instead of bread crumbs, here, when they poop, they shoot some missiles...

- In Italy we have (we had?) the crime of "fascist apology." No one can be fascist anymore. In Uzbekistan there is the crime of "communist apology".

- Piani, my surname, in Kazakh means "drunk" and this was my *passport* to enter the sympathies of many people. But it was also the condemnation of my liver.

- Gorbachev, Perestroika. The more I asked people the less I understood. The disgregation of the only nation where almost all of its ethnic minorities did not want independence. In Uzbekistan, for example, there was a referendum to ask people whether they preferred to stay with Russia or have independence. The first option won easily.

- Gorbachev part 2: the two/three presidents before him were murdered. Then he arrived, the Soviet Union collapsed and someone made a lot of money. Was he a real Nobel Prize for peace or just a puppet?

- In Kazakhstan, a litre of gasoline costs less than a litre of water. Considering that cycling meant I needed to drink five/six liters of water a day, maybe it would have been more convenient for me to travel by car.

- When I was pedaling in a remote area and was suddenly assaulted by a swarm of flies, it often meant that there was a flock of sheep or cows nearby. In those case, when there was a flock, there was also a big sheepdog. So, the equation was simple: flies = start pedaling fast before it gets too late!

- I have always wondered why all the sports clubs of the "Soviet area" have the same names: Cska, Lokomotiv, Dynamo... this is because during communism, since there was no private property, the teams could not be owned by one person or by a private company, as in Europe so they were owned by state organisations. So, Lokomotiv is the team of railwaymen, Dynamo is the police team and army's team is Cska.

- Tashkent, the Uzbek capital, was born in the Second World War. Hitler's Germany arrived in Stalingrad and the Soviet Union had to move all its war production away from Nazis coming from the west and Japanese coming from the east. So, some small agricultural towns in Central Asia were suddenly transformed into the largest concentrated war industry. Tashkent was one of these towns.

- One day while I was pedalling, pretty tired, over a hill, two guys approached me on horseback. They looked at my bike and asked me "Skolka?" - how much? I told them it's a cheap Chinese bike, 300 US dollars. They looked at each other and started laughing, pointing at the horse and saying: "200 dollars!!!".

- On the way to Samarcanda I stopped to sleep in a wood. The next morning at a crossroad I could not remember is the way to the main road. An old man passed by on a donkey cart and I asked him, "Samarkand?". He pointed to the right direction, while a thrill of emotion paralyses me on the pedals. What's more magical for a traveller, than asking for directions to Samarcanda while you're going there with your own two legs?

- Scorpions of the desert in Uzbekistan seem to like Colgate toothpaste. Every morning, when I got out of my tent, I always found two or three of them around my spit from the previous evening.

- I have seen many different *genetic mix* in my travels, but the color of the eyes that some people have in Karakalpakstan, a western province of Uzbekistan, is magnificent. They have shining yellow eyes. When I met these people in the street I just couldn't stop staring at their eyes.

- If I stopped every time someone offered me a sip of vodka, I would have arrived in Italy in 2024... Or maybe I would never have arrived.

- Less than thirty years after the fall of the Soviet Union, the link between these "new republics" and Russia is still strong, despite the ever-increasing involvement of China. The Russian nuclear warheads are probably still somewhere in Kazakhstan, while in Uzbekistan, the former president Karimov (who died two years ago), practically gave away the country's gas fields to Yeltsin, the president of Russia, who helped him take control of the country.

- In the collective imagination, Samarcanda is the center of the *Silk Road*. In reality, the city of Bukhara was the real cornerstone, exactly halfway between Europe and China. During my first visit two years ago, it did not strike me so much, ruined by the countless shops selling souvenirs. This time, however, I decided to use the technique I used in India to protect myself from the heat - sleeping during the day and being a tourist at night, this time trying to faithfully re-experience what the merchant's caravans had to find in the Middle Ages. Silence, the moonlit mosques and the tiny dusty streets, brought me back in time into a magical atmosphere.

- Travelling by bike forced me to go to absolutely non-tourist locations (where local people didn't see me like a walking dollar) and this allowed me to get to know people deeply. The hospitality and kindness of the Uzbeks was a pleasant surprise!

- Central Asia always manages to amaze me - an incredible mix of ethnic groups and religions who live peacefully without caring about who has the Islamic hijab, who has almond shape eyes, who speaks only Russian or who is a nomad. I was talking to a Kazakh girl, telling her how in Europe we are more "sensitive" about ethnic differences. She answered me "Here it's fine... we are too lazy to create useless problems!" Right, useless problems...

THIRD TRIP REPORT
OCTOBER - NOVEMBER 2018

Nations crossed: eastern Kazakhstan, Caspian Sea, Azerbaijan and Georgia

0 flat tires (since I changed them in Urumqi, five thousand kilometers ago)

1 night spent under the ferries wheel of an abandoned playground in Azerbaijan

2 spokes of the front wheel repaired by myself... successfully

3 nights spent in cemeteries

4° the lowest temperature at which I cycled

11 euro, the average daily amount spent in Azerbaijan. Nothing considering that I almost always slept in the hostels

30 hours of navigation to cross the Caspian Sea

50+ cups of tea offered to me in two weeks by locals

54 km/h the speed of the opposite wind that I suffered in the Kazakh steppe

300 km cycled in the steppe without meeting any village

6100 km traveled so far, from China to Tbilisi, capital of Georgia

Some considerations on the places visited:

- In the small villages and towns in the Kazakh steppe, until not long ago there was the custom that man, helped by his friends, could "kidnap" a girl from the village, take her to his home where there were all his family waiting for them, and marry her without her consent. Now, thirty years later, in the same villages and cities there is an "explosion" of divorces.

- As soon as I entered Azerbaijan I withdrew the local currency. I typically withdrew the maximum available, so this time it was 200 manats, which I received in two 100 bills. After riding about thirty kilometres I stopped in a shop and bought a Coca Cola, a juice, two packs of biscuits and an ice cream, the total price 2,5 manat (1,40 €). I gave the 100 manat bill to the merchant who, waving his hand made me understand he does not have the change. I was about to put the goods back on the shelves and go away, but I was stopped by the truck driver behind me at the counter, who mumbled something and paid all my expenses ...

- Tbilisi, the capital of Georgia, is really cool! Upon arriving there I heard people calling it the "new Berlin" for its numerous and massive artistic and cultural events, The "Melbourne of the Caucasus" for its relaxed and chilled atmosphere, The "New York of the East" for its multiculturality...

- The artistic heritage of the Kazakh cities of the west part is much lower than the artistic heritage of Buccinasco and Cinisello Balsamo (two towns near Milano well known for being pretty ugly).

- In Azerbaijan there is a "curious democracy". The current president came to power after the death of his predecessor... who was his own father... I guess it sounds more like a "monarchy".

- I have no knowledge to talk about vaccines, but all "no-vax" people against mandatory vaccines should take a look in central Asia and some Chinese areas where young boys or some couples cannot live a normal life and engage in sexual activity because they are infected by some of those diseases that in the Western countries we almost do not even remember because they don't exist anymore thanks to mandatory vaccines.

- In Kazakhstan, camels from breeding are distinguished from the wild ones because the farmers engrave a cross or a letter on their neck or belly to recognize them. Just outside the city of Beyneu I came across a camel that had on its belly written "CK", with the same characters used for the Calvin Klein logo.

- The mayor of Tbilisi is Kakha Kaladze. Yes, the former AC Milan football player. I waited for him just outside the municipality to tell him that I had bought him at the *Football Fantasy* in 2011 when he played in Genoa, but I didn't meet him. Seriously, the Georgians I have met are almost all enthusiastic about his work.

- In Azerbaijan, a *Doner Kebab* costs between 0.4 and 0.7 eurocents... Guess how many can I eat after eight hours cycling!

- In Kazakhstan, the visceral passion for "Made in Italy" means that many boutiques have Italian names. I saw creepy clothing stores called Armani and Versace, but also Berlusconi (our former prime minister) and Balotelli (the most stupid Italian football player ever).

- For about two years, between the Zar empire and the USSR, Tbilisi was simultaneously the capital of Georgia, Armenia and Azerbaijan. This gives the city an incredible architectural heritage and a massive cultural diversity.

- Cycling alone in the desert or in the steppe is undoubtedly something self-destructive.

- Baku, capital of Azerbaijan, is the picture of what oil and gas can do. The capital of a "poor country" built in the image of Milan, Paris and St. Tropez. Pleasant, elegant and beautiful but incredibly false and contradictory.

- In Azerbaijan at least three, four times a day I was stopped by people who offered me a cup of tea. Here they have the custom of sipping it with a sugar cube in their mouth. They usually eat a couple of cubes per cup. It was a bit different for me. After all day riding, I never drank a cup of tea with less than eight sugar cubes.

- The face of the former Azerbaijan president (dictator?) is everywhere in the streets and public buildings - posters, monuments, statues. I saw some people with the president's face on their car dashboard and as a phone screensaver.

- In many restaurants and bars that serve tea in Azerbaijan (especially in the villages), there is no bathroom for women. Indeed, women in restaurants and tea bars are hardly ever seen.

- Tombs in Islamic cemeteries do not have tombstones like ours. They are huge blocks of cubic stone where the dead body is placed. In the Kazakh steppe they were the only shelter where I could pitch my tent, undisturbed by the wind and prying eyes. The first time I slept next to

Timur's tomb, a young man who died at the beginning of the century and was buried in the largest tomb of the cemetery. That night I had a terrible nightmare that woke me up. I was dreaming that my water supplies were finished so I got out of my tent to check the water bottles on the bike. Millions of bright dots surrounded me from every side of the horizon. There was not even an inch of sky that it was not occupied by a star. The bottles were full. I thanked Timur for having woken me up and I removed the tent cover to fall asleep looking at the stars.

FOURTH TRIP REPORT
NOVEMBER - DECEMBER 2018

Nations crossed: Georgia, Bulgaria, Serbia, Croatia, Slovenia and Italy

- 4° the lowest temperature at which I cycled

0 flat tyres since I put the new tyres on in Urumqi (7000 km ago)

4 flat tyres in the whole trip (all of them in the first month, before Urumqui)

5 espresso coffees that I drunk on my first day in Italy

6 days in Belgrade, the longest break of the trip... though the day I arrived I promised myself to leave Belgrade the next day

12 kg lost since I left China

84 days cycling during the trip

98.7 the average daily kilometres travelled

103 hours spent on the cargo ship to cross the Black Sea from Georgia to Bulgaria

139 days of travel from China to Italy

169 km the longest distance cycled in one day

2500+ euros collected for the Tashi Orphan School, the Nepalese orphanage that I sponsored through the trip

8295 the total km cycled from the northern border of Tibet to Milan

- We must start to re-evaluate the quality of products "Made in China". Over eight thousand kilometers cycled on some of the most devastated roads on the planet, and my Chinese bike, which I paid 200 euros for, and all my equipment never had a serious problem.

- On the third night on the cargo boat on the black sea, the chef on board approached me and told me "Hey, Italian! Tomorrow is Sunday, I cook macaroni!". I celebrate, after three days of chicken and soup, unaware that the macaroni will be served the next day at 7.30 as breakfast. Cooked for at least forty-five minutes and served with ketchup or mayonnaise or mustard instead of proper tomato sauce. In Italy, something like that would be forbidden by law. Don't joke about Pasta!

- The Georgian alphabet, in Georgian "ქართული დამწერლობა," is officially, among all the world alphabets, the most similar to the one engraved on the *Lord of the Rings* ring.

- The Georgian alphabet, as well as its language, is one of the oldest in the world. The Georgians are so proud of it that all the international brands are obliged to write the name with both Latin and Georgian characters on their shop signs. In Tbilisi I saw the names of any brand, from McDonald's to Versace and Nike, translated into Georgian. All of them, except Armani Jeans... Armani Jeans was not translated.

- Georgian cuisine is really delicious but unluckily it is a huge mixture of fat and carbohydrates. The Khachapuri, one of the typical dishes, is a kind of thick italian focaccia, filled with different types of cheese and herbs. It is always served with a half-cooked egg on the surface and a cube of butter melting on top.

- Since the governament legalised marijuana in Georgia, the three-days crossing the Black Sea is much more enjoyable for Georgian and Bulgarian sailors. If there is also an Armenian truck driver with a load of Armenian Brandy, the real party can start.

- Stalin was Georgian. I remembered when I was crossing the town of Gori and, riding my bike, I accidentally came across the museum dedicated to him. It was impossible from that moment on not to smile at every person with the black mustache that I met in the street... almost everyone.

- One of the last nights in Georgia, after cycling about 130 km, I stopped in a small town on the mountains. The sun had almost set and it had started getting cold, so I decided to look for a guest house instead of pitching my tent. According to my map there was one not too far away. Not finding any sign or indication, I rang the bell of the only building looked like it could be a guest house. No one answered, but the gate was open so I entered to call the owner. I walked to the house entrance, where I was welcomed by three hunting dogs crouched on the door, who, as soon as they saw me, started chasing me without the slightest sign of mercy. I turned immediately and ran to the exit where my bike was parked, but in the bustle I hit a huge metal cube that, falling to the ground, split into several pieces. I stopped to look at the mess I'd made and even the dogs stopped running and looked at me, confused. For two seconds we are all frozen, looking at each other. Then, from the broken box, hundreds of bees start flying out, quite angry because someone had just destroyed their house. They attacked the dogs, while I kept running to my bike and started cycling away as fast as possible, probably setting the new world record for the five kilometers distance.

- One of the first terrorist attacks in human history happened in Sofia, the capital of Bulgaria. The roof of the main church was filled with explosives, ready to explode during the religious ceremony where the king and all other high state officials were expected to attend. Almost everyone died, except for the king itself, the main target of the attack, because he showed up late. Since then in Bulgaria being late does not seem to be considered a problem.

- In Sofia, travelling with a low budget, I settled on one of the cheapest hostels in the city. Although on *Booking* it had decent reviews, a few hours were enough to understand that in reality the hostel was the den of local crime. On the first night while I was cooking a plate of pasta, a couple of guys entered the hostel's kitchen and, showing me a tiny amount of cocaine, they told me to get out of the kitchen because they had to do "their stuff". The pasta was almost ready to be served *"Al dente"* and, after a hundred kilometres ridden in the snow, I did not feel like eating badly cooked pasta. So, I told him with a pissed face that I like pasta al dente and would not leave the kitchen. I must have been quite convincing because not only did they leave the room, but they also apologized. Don't mess with an Italian man cooking Italian Pasta!

- In Serbia there is an old religious tradition called Slava. Each family is assigned their own Saint and, the day of the year in which that Saint is celebrated the family takes as a holyday with the right not to go to work or to school.

- The only country allied with the Nazis, who refused to deport the Jews present on its territory, was Bulgaria.

- One evening in Belgrade I went out with my friend Marko. He took me to the most famous place in the city where Milica Pavlovic, a sort of Serbian Katy Perry, sang for the occasion. The dress code included Armani's shirt and elegant shoes, while I'm practically dressed as a cyclist! None of the bouncers tried to stop me… Marko is a former basketball player, two meters and five with one hundred and twenty kilograms of muscle.

- One time, the first time since I started cycling from China, I got lost, ending unexpectedly in Temska, a tiny village on the Serbian mountains with fewer than 500 people. I reached the village totally wet and cold but mostly unmotivated, not knowing which way to go. A motorbike approached me, driven by a man in his fifties, who was obviously the local mailman. He introduced himself as Zelicko and without speaking English told me to follow him. After a few minutes I was in the village post office, where, as well as being seated near the heater, I got a glass of Slivovica (a Serbian spirit, 45 percent alcohol, home-made stuff) and some pastries. Tanjia, the office employee, even called the village doctor who joined us shortly after with the hospital nurse, as the only two people who speak English. They kept me company while I dried my feet on the radiator and above all they went shopping, buying me a bottle of Slivovica, a sandwich with a big piece of pork (half a kilo at least, I am not joking) and salami.

- On the morning of December 11th, the alarm was not necessary. I woke up much earlier, as excited as when I was a child on the morning of December 25th, when I went to see if Santa had really come to deliver the gifts. From Postojna in Slovenia to Italy, thirty-five kilometers, cycled singing and screaming to reach the most desired border... home's border, the most beautiful place in the world!!! After 469 days of which I spent 134 riding my bike travelling 7804 km, I was back in Italy. Then it was time for a decent *Espresso* in the Trieste central square before the final rush to Milan.

THE END

On December 16th, 2018 my journey by bicycle from China to Milan ended and with it my third crossing of the Asian continent over land. I also finished, for now, writing my reports, which I decided to collect in this book, to be able to tell, in a fun way, some Asian curiosities and features, seen through the eyes of a curious young traveler eager to mix with local people and to deepen the knowledge about different cultures and natural beauties. All anecdotes reported in this book are the description of facts that really happened to me on the road. Every comment, event, description and story are based on truth that I experienced and the information that I was told by local people regarding their traditions, religion and socio-political situations. I have always tried to maintain maximum impartiality regarding political and religious topics, always trying to listen to as many people as possible in order to get a precise and complete idea of the reality. This has not always been easy, especially in countries where English is poorly spoken or where dictatorial regimes limit freedom of expression. I tried to do my best, deepening some research, using other sources in order to make every comment as objective, truthful and respectful as possible.

Thus, ends another incredible journey! I'm happy to be back home, the most beautiful country in the world, surrounded by fantastic family and special friends. But my mind is already focused on the next trips... to my next adventures.

I meet many acquaintances and friends in the street. Some seem in awe before this person who they believe they do not know anymore. Many others, however, ask me how my journeys have changed me. I never know what to answer, although I know precisely how I grew up and changed during these years on the road. I just answer that the trip forced me to listen to myself, making me more aware of who I really am and consequently teaching me to accept myself and to live any experience in a more balanced way.

I also feel more aware of something equally precious; the beauty of the world and its wonderful people.

THANKS TO

Thanks to Ilaria and Federica, who helped me writing the book. It would have been much harder to write this book without their creativity and literary knowledge.

Thanks to Playdesign for editing the book and designing the cover. They made it for free, embracing the charity goal of the book.

Thanks to Mon, Jia Li and Julia. I would have never been able to translate the book from Italian to English without their help and corrections

Thanks to Elisabetta,Timur, Zelicko, Shynara, Marat, Monica, Mark, Aruna, Bolto, Maurizio, Tenzin, Jia Li, Anastasia, Abdoul, Sadeq, Luba, Ana, Zeynep and hundreds of other persons I have met on the road in the past four years... Real people, who opened to me their hearts and their houses just in exchange of a smile.

CPSIA information can be obtained
at www.ICGtesting.com
Printed in the USA
LVHW081500241020
669735LV00006B/321

9 781074 730819